100

Diseases Treated by Single Point of Acupuncture and Moxibustion

Written by
Chen Decheng

English Text Revised by
Linda Gale Sampson
Cynthia J. Chan

Foreign Languages Press   Beijing

First Edition 2001

Website:
http://www.flp.com.cn

Email Addresses:
Info@flp.com.cn
Sales@flp.com.cn

ISBN 7-119-02744-1
©Foreign Languages Press, Beijing, China, 2001

Published by Foreign Languages Press
24 Baiwanzhuang Road, Beijing 100037, China
Distributed by China International Book Trading Corporation
35 Chegongzhuang Xilu, Beijing 100044, China
P.O. Box 399, Beijing, China

Printed in the People's Republic of China

Foreword

Chinese acupuncture and moxibustion is an essential component of traditional Chinese medicine and has a long history. The single point therapy has an important position in acupuncture and moxibustion. It refers to the use of a single point of acupuncture and moxibustion to treat and prevent diseases.

The single point therapy has the characteristics of good curative effects, a wide range of indications, simple application, low cost, safety and easy acceptance by the patients.

I published the book *The Chinese Single Point Acupuncture and Moxibustion* in China in 1992. The book becomes very popular and has been accepted by the general readers at home and abroad. Now I choose some of the methods, which are of good results, simple manipulation, easy to study and use, to compile this book.

This book consists of five chapters: painful diseases, internal diseases, surgical diseases, obstetrical, gynecological and pediatric diseases, and ophthalmic and E.N.T. diseases, 100 diseases in total. The book has a wide range of indications and is useful for clinic.

The book has a unified style throughout the book. In each disease, the point, location, method, result, case and discussion are introduced.

I am deeply indebted to Egyptian Doctor Aly Bayomy who works at the Cairo University and to Mrs. Ye Brathaver for their support during the writing of the book.

Dr. Chen Decheng
in Beijing, China
March 2000

Contents

Chapter I
Painful Diseases

1.1. Headache

Headache is a subjective symptom that may appear in many acute and chronic diseases. The headache stated here refers to that as a main symptom in many exogenous or miscellaneous internal diseases. Headache can be seen in many infection diseases with fever in Western medicine such as hypertension, intracranial disease, psychoneurosis and migraine etc.

Point

Fengchi (GB 20)

Location

Fengchi (GB 20) acupoint is located on the nape, below the occipital bone, on the level of Fengfu (DU 16), in the depression between the upper ends of sternocleidomastoid and trapezius muscles (See Fig. 1).

Methods

1. Acupressure is used. With the patient in the sitting position, use the thumb and middle fingers of the right hand to manipulate Fengchi (GB 20) point on both sides by pressure and/or rolling, fingers around Fengchi (GB 20) point on both sides first mildly and then gradually increase power of pressure or rolling.

The procedure should be done for 10-15 minutes and repeat daily for 7 days.

2. Electroacupuncture is used. With the patient in the sitting position, use 2 needles of 1.5 *cun* long each. A needle is inserted at each Fengchi (GB 20) point with the direction towards the opposite ear and the depth is 1.2-1.3 *cun*. Manipulate each needle until the patient feels the arrival of *qi* sensation. Apply the electric machine using continuous frequency waveform for 20-30 minutes. One course constitutes 10 treatments.

3. Acupoint injection is used. With the patient in the sitting position, use 5 ml syringe containing 2 ml of vitamin B_1, 2 ml of 0.5% lidocaine and 1 ml of vitamin B_{12} is injected at the acupoint Fengchi (GB 20) on each side, with the needle directed towards the opposite ear and inserted at a depth of 2.5 cm. Once you reach this depth pull the handle of the syringe to make sure that no blood comes out, then push the fluid while withdrawing the needle. Usually one injection on each side is enough. If you don't get good results, repeat this after 2-3 days.

Results

1. *Method No.1:* 56 cases were treated with the duration of headache varying from one to more than five years. 43 cases had functional headache, 10 cases had hypertensive headache, and 3 cases had dysmenorrhoea headache. 36 cases were completely cured, 19 cases improved and no effect was found in one case. All cases needed no more than two courses of treatment.

2. *Method No.2:* 260 cases with headache due to sinusitis and drug intake were treated by this method. 258 cases were completely cured and 2 cases showed no improvement after one course of treatment.

3. *Method No.3:* 50 cases with severe chronic headache due

to head injury, trigeminal neuralgia, intracranial apace occupying lesion were treated by this method. 28 cases were completely cured, 14 cases improved and no effect was found in one case. All responding cases needed up to 4 sessions of treatment.

Cases

1. Lai xx, male, 9 years old, student, presented with severe headache of 6 months duration, and clinical examination and brain C.T. scan were normal. His headache improved on the first session of treatment and disappeared after the 5th session.

2. Ye xx, female, 56 years old, officer, presented with severe temporal headache of 10 years duration, increasing on exposure to cold and overstrain. After 3 sessions of acupuncture, the pain was relieved.

3. Tan xx, male, 41 years old, teacher, had a traffic accident with head injury 6 months earlier. He remained comatose for 5 days after the accident. He had severe headache with nausea and vomiting onset. Headache remained until time of presentation. The patient was injected every other day for 3 times, after three treatments, His pain vanished.

Discussion

1. The three methods are used in different headaches. The acupressure is suitable for mild cases, the electro-acupuncture is for moderate headache, and the point injection is for severe headache.

2. Fengchi (GB 20) acupoint is very rich in nerve supply, located close to important muscles of neck, head and main intracranial vessels and nerves. All the methods used improve *qi* and blood flow and around Fengchi (GB 20) acupoint, thus alleviating headache.

1.2. Pain in Supraorbital Area

Supraorbital pain is a kind of pain in forehead or supraorbiral bone, also a part of headache syndrome or migraine syndrome. Pain is usually accompanied by local soreness, photophobia and teary. It is least severe in the morning, most intense in the afternoon and decreases severity again at the evening.

Point
Kunlun (BL 60)

Location

Kunlun (BL 60) acupoint is located in the depression between the posterior border of the external malleolus and Achilles' tendon (See Fig. 2). At the same level is the tip of the malleolus.

Method

Acupuncture is used. Select the point on the affected side. Use a 1.5 *cun* needle, insert it quickly to a depth of up to 1 *cun* and manipulate it (using reinforcing method in long standing cases and reducing method in acute cases) until the patient gets *qi* sensation up to the knee. Retain the needle for 20-30 minutes and repeat manipulation every five minutes if pain recurs.

Result

16 cases were treated by this method. 15 cases were completely cured. Of the 15 cases, 10 cases were cured on one session treatment, 3 cases were on 2-3 sessions treatment and 2 cases were cured on 3-4 sessions treatment.

Case

Wang xx, male, 45 years old, officer, presented supraorbital pain, which was most intense in the afternoon. He was treated by this method. During needling, pain was relieved after 15 minutes. Pain did not recur after the second session.

Discussion

This type of pain usually starts in the morning. The best results can be obtained if the needle is inserted about 1/2 hour before the expected onset of pain. If pain is chronic, using press needles can control this situation.

1.3. Migraine

Migraine is a kind of common headache. This disease is usually related to inheritance, and may occur repeatedly with the first attack in childhood. It is often induced by seasonal pathogenic factors, such as over fatigue, tension, excitement, poor sleep or menstrual period. There are repeated attacks of intolerable burning, throbbing or boring pain on the forehead, temple and obit unilaterally in most cases and bilaterally in few cases. The pain usually lasts for a few minutes or even 1-2 days. Sometime it attacks several times a day. It may reattack in few months or few years.

Point 1
Yifeng (SJ 17)

Location

Yifeng (SJ 17) acupoint is located posterior to the ear lobe, in the depression between the mastoid process and mandibular angle (See Fig. 3).

Method

Electroacupuncture is used. Use a 2 *cun* needle, insert the needle at a depth of 1.5 *cun* directed towards the contra lateral point. Manipulate the needle by rotating and lifting techniques, using more the rotating method. Most patients feel *qi* sensation arriving up to the throat and root of the tongue, if the needle is inserted deep enough, if pain is so severe. Apply also to the opposite side and connect to the electric machine, using continuous waveform for 20-30 minutes.

Result

150 cases were treated by this method. 76 cases were completely cured, 56 cases were markedly improved, 14 cases were improved and no effect was obtained in 4 cases. Total effective rate was 97.33%.

Case

Wen xx, female, 49 years old, farmer, presented her left side migraine for 10 years. The migraine was accompanied by nausea, vomiting and irritability. TCM diagnosis was migraine due to stagnation of *qi* and blood. The patient was treated by this method, and started to have improvement after the first session. She obtained complete relief after 10 sessions.

Discussion

Migraine is Shaoyang headache, which belongs to Sanjiao Meridian. So we use Yifeng (SJ 17) acupoint, because it belongs to Sanjiao Meridian of Hand in local area. It is special for migraine. It improves *qi* and blood flow in cervical, cranial nerves and vessels, thus relieving migraine.

Point 2
Reaction point (Vesicle form)

Location
Vesicle form can be found in some cases of migraine, on both sides of spinous processes of cervical spine. This vesicle is small, white, light red or gray in color. It is palpable, and doesn't disappear with pressure.

Method
Three-edged needle is used. If vesicle is seen, use the needle to remove it, making a break through the skin and fiber. Repeat this for 3-5 times, and then apply local anti-inflammatory drugs. Cover with plaster. Don't repeat procedure.

If you don't see the vesicle, rub with your fingers until you feel their site. If still not detected it, then make your cuts at Dingchuan (EX-B1) extra point.

Result
30 cases with migraine were treated by this method and gave good results.

Case
Yin xx, female, 40 years old, worker. She had migraine with one-year history, accompanied by dizziness, dry mouth and insomnia. The vesicle was found between the 3rd and 4th cervical spine and 0.5 *cun* from the spine. After cutting it, the migraine was improved and disappeared after one week.

Discussion
For each disease there is specific external signs. Vesicle is

specific for migraine, cutting it to regulate and improve brain functions.

1.4. Trigeminal Neuralgia

Trigeminal Neuralgia is characterized by sudden attacks of spasmodic electric shock-like severe pain in the facial areas, supplied by the trigeminal nerve, ophthalmic, maxillary and mandibular divisions (mainly along the maxillary and mandibular divisions). Attacks may recur several times daily, generally when the patient is washing the face, brushing the teeth, eating or walking.

Point 1
Tinggong (SI 19) (For Maxillary and Trigeminal Pain)

Location

Tinggong (SI 19) acupoint is located on the face, anterior to the tragus and posterior to the mandibular condyloid process, in the depression found when the mouth is open (See Fig. 4).

Method

Acupuncture is used. Select the point on the affected side, use a 1.5 *cun* needle, number 30, insert the needle for 1 *cun*, and manipulate until the patient feels *qi* sensation arriving on the same side, retain the needle for up to one hour in severe cases, without manipulation. But if after the first 30 minutes pain is not relieved, you can repeat manipulation every 10 minutes for the next 30 minutes.

Result

63 cases were treated by this method. 44 were completely cured, 11 were improved and 8 cases showed improvement but with recurrence of pain after one year.

Case

Li xx, male, 70 years old, worker, had right facial pain of 5 days with no improvement by Western medical treatment. He showed markedly improvement after 3 minutes during the treatment, when the needle was further retained for one hour. After 3 sessions, he had no more pain.

Discussion

This point is special for maxillary and trigeminal pain.

Point 2

Yangbi (GB 14) (For Ophthalmic Pain)

Location

Yangbai (GB 14) acupoint is located on the forehead, directly above the pupil, 1 *cun* above the eyebrow (See Fig. 5).

Method

Acupuncture is used. Select the point on the affected side. Use a 1.5 *cun* needle, insert it horizontally and inferior for 1 *cun* towards Yuyao (EX-HN 4) point, manipulate until the arrival of *qi* by using rotating method, and retain the needle for up to 30 minutes. Also you can use retained needle, covered with plaster to be removed the next day. Yuyao (EX-HN 4) point is in the middle of the eyebrow directly above the pupil.

1.5. Occipital Neuralgia

Occipital neuralgia refers to pain in the occipital and upper cervical areas, often caused by some infection conditions, neck sprain or changes in the cervical vertebrae from C_1 to C_4. Its main clinic manifestations are pain in the occipital area and upper cervical area, which is often induced by awkward movement of the neck, sneezing or cough. During the attack, the patient feels restricted in the neck and pain that is mostly continuous or aggravated in paroxysmal attacks. There may also be some sharp pain even when the attack is over.

Point
Fengchi (GB 20)

Location

Fengchi (GB 20) acupoint is located on the nape, below the occipital bone, on the level of Fengfu (DU 16) point, in the depression between the upper ends of sternocleidomastoid and trapezius muscles (See Fig. 1).

Method

Point injection is used. The patient is in the sitting position. Use 5 ml syringe containing 2 ml of vitamin B_1, 2ml of 0.5% lidocaine and 500 ug, 1ml of vitamin B_{12}, which is injected at the site of Fengchi (GB 20) point on each side, with the needle directed towards the opposite ear and inserted at a depth of 2.5 cm. Once you reach this depth, pull the handle of the syringe to make sure that no blood comes out, then push the fluid while withdrawing the needle. Usually one injection on each side is enough. If you don't get good results, repeat after 2-3 days.

Result

91 cases were treated by this method. 69 cases were completely cured, 20 cases were markedly improved after 1-3 treatments, 2 cases showed no effect after more than 3 treatments.

Case

Zhang xx, male, 48 years old, had pain in posterior head and neck for one month. The pain occurred while turning his head or when coughing. He took many Western medicines without effect. Tenderness of the Fengchi (GB 20) point was found in the examination. Diagnosis is occipital neuralgia. He was treated by this method and was completely cured after three treatments

Discussion

Fengchi (GB 20) acupoint is very rich in nerve supply, located close to important muscles of neck, head and main intracranial vessels and nerves. All the methods used improve *qi* and blood flow and around Fengchi (GB 20) point, thus alleviating headache.

1.6. Stiff Neck

Stiff neck refers to sprain of the neck muscles due to exposure to cold, sleeping on high pillow, excessive and prolonged tilting to one side. Usually it manifests with pain, stiffness and limited neck movement. One of two points can be used: Xuanzhong (GB 39) and Houxi (SI 3).

Point 1
Xuanzhong (GB 39)

Location

Xuanzhong (GB 39) acupoint is located on the lateral side of the leg, 3 *cun* above the tip of external malleolus, on the anterior border of fibula (See Fig. 6).

Method

Acupuncture is used. With the patient in the sitting position, expose the point bilaterally. Use a 1.5 to 2 *cun* needle, insert it 1.2 to 1.8 *cun*, depending on the size of the patient, and stimulate strongly until the patient feels a *qi* sensation going up to the knee. Meanwhile, the patient should exercise the neck muscles. Retain the needle for 15-20 minutes and repeat manipulation every five minutes.

Result

74 cases were treated by this method. 43 were completely cured (41 cases with one treatment and two cases with two treatments), 3 cases were improved with two treatments, and 1 case had no improvement.

Case

Zhao xx, male, 27 years old. He had right side neck pain due to poor sleeping position, with tenderness and stiffness of the neck muscles and inability to tilt the neck to the right side. Diagnosis was stiff neck. He was treated by this method. He showed little improvement with massage. After 20 minutes acupuncture treatment, he had much improved.

Discussion

Xuanzhong (GB 39) acupoint belongs to the gallbladder meridian, which flows through the neck. Inserting the needle at

Xuanzhong (GB 39) point improves *qi* and blood flow along the gallbladder meridian, thus alleviating pain and neck stiffness.

Point 2
Houxi (SI 3)

Location
Houxi (SI 3) acupoint is located at the junction of the red and white skin along the ulnar border of the hand, at the ulnar end of the distal palmar crease, proximal to the 5th metacarpophalangeal joint when a hollow fist is made (See Fig. 7).

Method
Acupuncture is used. With the patient in the sitting position, select the point on both sides. Use a 1.5 *cun* needle, inserted towards Hegu (LI 4) point, at a depth of more than 1 *cun*. Rotate the needle using the reducing method for 1-3 minutes until the patient feels no more pain. Then remove the needle. If pain is not relieved, retain the needle for 20-30 minutes and repeat manipulation every five minutes.

Result
54 cases were treated by this method. 33 cases were completely cured, 19 cases improved and 2 cases showed no improvement. Most of the improved cases needed 1-2 sessions of treatment.

Case
Xao xx, male, 37 years old. He came to the clinic with morning neck stiffness. His pain radiated to the right side of the shoulder and tilted neck to the left side. Diagnosis is stiff neck.

He was treated by this method. His pain was relieved with three minutes manipulation.

1.7. Cervical spondylopathy

Cervical spondylopathy refers to the condition in which hyperosteogeny of the cervical vertebra stimulates or oppresses the cervical nerve root, spinal cord, vertebral artery or sympathetic nerve, causing pain and limited movement or other symptoms. The main clinic manifestations are soreness, distension or pain of the neck, shoulder or arm, numbness of the fingers, etc. It is usually seen in those at the age over forty.

Point
Changshanxia (Experience Point)

Location
Changshanxia (experience point) is located two *cun* below the point Chengshan (BL 57), a little to the inner side, according to the site of tenderness. [Shengsan (BL 57) point is located on the posterior midline of the leg, between Weizhong (BL 40) point and Kunlun (BL 60) point, in a pointed depression formed below the gastrocnemius muscle belly when the leg is stretched or the heel is lifted] (See Fig. 8).

Method
Acupuncture, cupping and massage are used. With the patient in the prone position, localize the point on both sides, according to local tenderness. Insert the needle perpendicularly for 1.5 *cun* and manipulate until the patient feels a *qi* sensation. Then, cover the needle with a cup. After 15 minutes, remove the

needle and the cup and start massage, first using both hands to make all leg muscles relaxed. Continue massage with the thumb around the local area, to run the point up the leg. Repeat rubbing up to 20-30 minutes, until the patient's neck feels hot, with a distending sensation and sweating. The patient should exercise his neck during the entire treatment.

Result

The patient needs 10 or more treatments to be cured.

Case

Luo xx, male, 45 years old, presented neck pain and numbness in both hands. On inserting needles, Luo felt a hot stream from the low back, up to the neck, shoulder and hand, with sweating. He found steady improvement, until complete relief was obtained after 10 sessions.

1.8. Periarthritis of Shoulder

Periarthritis of shoulder is a chronic, retrograde and inflammatory disease of the shoulder joint, capsule and the soft tissues around it, mostly due to exposure to cold trauma and chronic strain of the shoulder. The main clinic manifestations are soreness and dysfunction of the shoulder. The disease is usually found in people at the age of 50 or more.

Point

Tiaokou (ST 38)

Location

Tiaohou (ST 38) acupoint is located on the anteriolateral

side of the leg, 8 *cun* below Dubi (ST 35) point, and one finger breadth (middle finger) from the anterior crest of tibia (See Fig. 9).

Methods

1. Acupuncture is used. With the patient in the sitting position, puncture point on the affected side, using a 1.5-2.5 *cun* needle, stimulate the point strongly by lifting and rotating method for about 3 minutes until the patient gets sense of *qi* sensation. Retain the needle for 20 minutes during which the manipulation is repeated 2-3 times. Repeat sessions every 1-2 days till the patient can move shoulder actively without pain.

2. Piercing needling therapy is used. With the patient in the sitting position, expose Tiaokuo (ST 38) point on the affected side. Use needle number 26 or 28 (thick needle), 3-4 *cun* long. Insert the needle at Tiaokuo (ST 38) point directed forwards Chengshan (BL 57) point, to a depth of 2.5-3.5 *cun*. Manipulate the needle, rotating anticlockwise until the patient feels *qi* sensation going up the arm and shoulder, meanwhile the patient moves his shoulder joint in any direction. Once sensation is obtained, the needles are retained for 15 minutes, during this period the procedure is repeated for 2-3 times. Repeat sessions every 1-2 days.

3. Point injection is used. Use a 5ml syringe containing 1 ml of Vitamin B_{12}, 2ml of 0.5% lidocaine and 1 ml of Vitamin B_1, at the point Tiaokuo (ST 38) or bilaterally inject 2 ml of the mixture at a depth of 2 cm (even if shoulder pain is unilateral). Repeat the procedure for 1-2 times per week. At the same time apply flash cupping at Ashi points of shoulder.

Results

1. 34 cases were treated by the first method. 13 cases were completely cured, 16 cases were markedly improved, 3 cases were improved and 2 cases showed no change.

2. 45 cases were treated by the second method, 38 cases were completely cured, 3 cases were improved and 4 cases showed no effect.

3. 53 cases were treated by the third method for 1-3 weeks, and all gave good result.

Cases

1. Wang xx, male, 52 years old, officer, presented with pain in right shoulder and limited movement. TCM diagnosed as periarthritis of shoulder due to wind and damp. He received many drugs and applied local strapping with no effect. He was treated by the first method. He had been completely cured after four treatments.

2. Gao xx, female, 52 years old, female, presented with right shoulder pain, accompanied by limitation of movement of two months duration. Mrs. Gao was treated by the second method. She had markedly improved after the first treatment and had no more pain after four sessions.

3. Huang xx, female, 54 years old, presented with chronic right shoulder pain of 10 years. Diagnosis was periarthritis of the shoulder. She received many drugs with no effect, and was treated by the third method, point injection for 6 times had much improved her complaint.

Discussion

1. The point Tiaokuo (ST 38) belongs to Stomach Meridian of Yangming. Yangming Meridians are the richest in *qi* and

blood flow among the 12 regular meridians. Tiaokuo (ST 38) stimulation can make blood and *qi* flow efficiently in the Stomach Meridian up to the shoulder. Active shoulder movement relieves stagnation of blood and encourages flow of *qi* thus relieving pain and limitation of movement.

2. The needle may be inserted at Tiaokuo (ST 38) point or at a point around Tiaokuo (ST 38), but not more than 1 *cun* from this point. The side of it is actually the most painful tenderness point. Both sides should be checked for the most painful point.

3. The point Tiaokuo (ST 38) is the only point with referred tenderness in shoulder joint diseases among all the points discovered until now.

4. Between acupuncture sessions, the patient should exercise the shoulder actively at home for 30 minutes, 2-3 times daily.

1.9. Brachialgia

Brachialgia refers to pain more marked in shoulder than arm and elbow followed by motor weakness. Sensory loss is usually minimal. It is due to brachial plexus injury by traction, penetrating wounds or compression. The upper part of the brachial plexus is commonly more affected than the lower part.

Point
Futu (LI 18)

Location
Futu (LI 18) acupoint is located on the lateral side of the neck, beside the laryngeal protuberance, between the anterior and posterior borders of sternocleidonastiod muscle (See Fig. 10).

Method

Acupuncture is used. Use the point on the affected side. A 1 *cun* needle is inserted at the point directed towards the cervical spine to a depth not more than 0.5 *cun* to avoid injury of the carotid artery. Once the patient feels *qi* sensation down to the arm, remove the needle. Do not retain it. Repeat daily for up to 10 days.

Result

123 cases were treated by this method. 92 cases were completely cured, 26 cases were improved and 5 cases did not improved.

Case

Shu xx, male, 59 years old, farmer, who developed left shoulder and arm pain on exposure to rainy weather with marked limitation of arm movement. Diagnosis is brachialgia. He was treated by this method. His pain was markedly improved after five treatments. By the end of the 7th treatment, he could move his arm freely.

Discussion

The point Futu (LI 18) belongs to the Hand Yangming Meridian, which flows through the arm and around the shoulder. Stimulation of this point can improve *qi* and blood flow in shoulder and arm.

1.10. Tennis Elbow

"Tennis elbow" is also called lateral humeral epicondylitis, which manifests itself in pain in the origin of the common tendon of forearm extensors, on the lateral side of the elbow joint. The occurrence of this illness is caused by laceration, bleeding, adhesion or aseptic inflamamtory change in the general tendon of the extensor muscle, at the origin of the external epicondyle of the humerus due to chronic strain. It manifests itself in pain in the lateral side of the elbow, which can radiate to shoulder and wrist. The affected arm feels sore and weak. The illness is sometimes severe and sometimes attenuated.

Point
Ashi point

Location
This Ashi point is located in the center of the lateral humeral epicondyle.

Methods
1. Moxibustion is used. Moxibustion with ginger. Let the patient sit with his/her arm on the table and the elbow is flexed. Check for Ashi point around the elbow. Take a piece of fresh ginger and rub it around Ashi point until the local area of the skin becomes little red. Apply a small piece of Musk (a kind of Chinese drug, the size is similar to a piece of rice) on Ashi point. Cut a piece of ginger 0.3 *cun* thick and 3-4 *cun* in diameter, and cut a piece of plaster with a hole for the ginger, and fix it around ginger tightly so that no air can go inside through plaster edges. Ignite of the moxa and apply it as near as 3 *cun* from the ginger until the patient feels the local area comfortable and warm (not too hot). The session should last for 10 minutes. Keep plaster and ginger with the small piece of the musk for the next session, remove plaster and ginger, and repeat procedure session daily

for 10 days.

2. Intradermal needle is used. Use an intradermal needle with the handle about 0.5 *cun* long insert it horizontally at the Ashi point between the skin and muscle, in the direction of muscle fibers. Fix it by plaster, and ask the patient to exercise elbow until the patient feels comfortable without pain. Keep the needle retained for 3-5 days, then remove.

3. Dermal needle (plum-blossom needle or Seven-star needle) is used. Tap Ashi point until a few blood comes out, then apply moxa (as above) until the skin becomes red in color. Repeat this every other day until patient feels improvement.

Results

1. Mehtod 1: moxibustion with ginger. 100 cases were treated. 70 were completely cured, 17 were markedly improved, 15 were improved and 3 cases showed no effect.

2. Method 2: intradermal needle. 25 cases were treated. 16 were completely cured (12 cases on one session treatment, and 4 cases on two sessions treatment), and 9 cases were improved.

3. Method 3: dermal needle. 15 cases were treated, all were improved after 2-3 sessions.

Cases

1. Zhang xx, male, 38 years old, worker, presented with right elbow pain accompanied by pain and limitation of movement. Pain increased on effort and exposure to cold. Apply the first method for 3 courses treatment, and pain has markedly improved.

2. Feng xx, male, 58 years old, presented with right elbow pain for one month, and pain increased by moving elbow. Apply the second method, the needle was retained for 3 days, after

which he had marked improvement.

3. Peng xx, male, 23 years old, presented with right elbow pain of 5 days. Pain aggravated by movement. Apply the third method, and the condition improved after 2 sessions.

Discussion

The disease is due to overstraining of the joint or exposure to cold, both causing deficiency of *qi* and stagnation of blood, with subsequent pain and tenderness (Ashi point) and weakness of tendons and muscles. All the methods used promote *qi* flow and relieve stagnation of blood.

1.11. Sprain of Wrist and Ankle

Sprain of wrist and ankle refers to the sprain due to injury. Main clinic manifestations are pain, swelling and limitation of movement in local area.

Point

Relative point

Location

Relative point means that, if the ankle is injured, localize the site of Ashi point on it. The relative point is corresponding in location to Ashi point on the wrist. On contrary, if wrist is injured, select the relative point on Ashi point of some location of the ankle.

Method

Acupuncture is used. Select the relative point on the affected side. Use a 1 *cun* needle, insert it at relative point directed obliquely and proximally up for a depth up to 0.5-0.8 *cun*, manipulate the needle by reducing method, using lifting, thrusting and rotating techniques until the patient feels *qi* sensation. The patient should exercise the joint during procedure. The needle is retained for 20-30 minutes. If pain recurs, repeat manipulation very five minutes; for joint swelling, apply local anti-inflammatory drug and cover with plaster.

Result

40 cases (15 with wrist and 25 with ankle injury) were treated by this method. All of the cases had pain with swelling and limitation of joint movement. They were all improved after one treatment.

Case

Bai xx, male, 40 years old, officer, had his right ankle injured on the staircase. His ankle was swollen, painful with limitation of movement with normal X-ray film. Diagnosis was sprain of ankle. He was treated by this method. By manipulating the relative point on the right wrist for 15 minutes, the pain was much improved. After 3 sessions, there was no more complaint.

Discussion

Relative points are used far away from the lesion, because we do not know the nature of the hidden injury. Needle insertion at local area may exacerbate the hidden injury. The wrist and ankle are micro acupuncture therapy. They are related to each other through meridians and collaterals. So we may treat the pain at one joint by manipulation of the relative point on the other.

1.12. Shoulder and Back Pain

Shoulder and back pain refers to the pain in the back due to shoulder arthritis or local inflammation of tendons and muscles. Its main manifestations are limitation of movement and pain and tenderness over the affected area.

Point

Shangshandian (Experience Point)

Location

Draw a line three *cun* from the thyroid cartilage, then continue perpendicular downward for 1 *cun*. The point is inside the sternocleidomastiod muscle (See Fig. 11).

Method

Acupuncture is used. Select the point on the affected side. Use a 1.5 *cun*, with size number 28, needle. Insert the needle to a depth not more than 0.5 *cun* and lift and thrust quickly, use small amplitude until patient receives a *qi* sensation. The best effect is obtained, if patient feels *qi* sensation going down to fingers. Once *qi* sensation is felt, remove the needle, and do not retain needle.

Result

246 cases were treated by this method. 133 cases were completely cured, 122 cases were improved and 9 cases were not improved.

Case

Zhao xx, female, 59 years old, presented with hemiplegia of six months, accompanied by shoulder and back pain. She was treated by this method. The pain was improved after the first treatment. After 10 treatments her arm started to regain power.

1.13. Intercostal Neuralgia

Intercostal neuralgia is characterized by prickling or lancinating pain from the distribution region of the intercostal nerve. Main manifestations are frequent pain in one or more intercostal spaces, sometimes with a belt like distribution. Pain is intensified by coughing or deep breathing, and is characterized by a sharp pricking or electric shock sensation.

Point
   *Qi*uxu (GB 40)

Location
   *Qi*uxu (GB 40) acupoint is located anterior and inferior to the external malleolus, in the depression lateral to the tendon of long extensor muscle of toes (See Fig. 12).

Method
   Acupuncture is used. Use the point *Qi*uxu (GB 40) on the contra lateral side, a 1.5 *cun* needle is inserted to a depth of 1.0 *cun* and rotated till patient feels *qi* sensation. The needle is retained for 30 minutes with the manipulation repeated every 10 minutes. Repeat the treatment every day.

Result
   44 cases were treated by this method. 33 cases were completely cured, 8 cases were improved and 3 cases did not show any improvement. Most improving cases showed optimal effect

after 6 sessions.

Case

Yang xx, male, 17 years old, student, presented with burning right side chest, pain accompanied with tenderness on the mid-clavicular line from the 4th to the 6th rib and not responding to medical improvement. TCM diagnosis was intercostal neuralgia due to stagnation of blood. He started to have improvement after the first session and was completely cured after 8 sessions.

Discussion

Intercostal space belongs to Shaoyang Meridians. Qiuxu (GB 40) is one of the primary points of gall bladder of Shaoyang Meridian of Foot; manipulation of the point Qiuxu (GB 40) improves *qi* and blood flow thereby.

1.14. Lumbar Transverse Process Syndrome

Lumbar transverse process syndrome, also called the third lumbar transverse process inflammation, refers to muscle injury caused by aseptic swelling, hyperemia, exudation, etc. This leads to proliferation of periosteum, fibrous tissue. Clinic manifestations are pain in lower back, radiating to the leg on the same side, aggravated by movement.

Point
Ashi Point

Location

The Ashi point is located in the center of the painful area in the lumbar region.

Method

Acupuncture and cupping therapy are used. Patient lies down in a prone position with a small pillow beneath his/her abdomen. Select Ashi points on the affected side. Use a 3 *cun* needle, insert it strongly up to a depth of 2 *cun* and manipulate by the reducing method. Once the patient gets *qi* sensation, cover the needle with the cup and retain for 20 minutes. Repeat every other day; one course has 6 sessions.

Result

85 cases were treated by this method. 61 cases were completely cured, 22 cases were improved and 2 cases did not show any improvement.

Case

Zhou xx, male, 27 years old, soldier. On carrying his gun up the shoulder, he got low back pain, X-ray film showed L_3 transverse process injury. Diagnosis is lumbar vertebra number 3 transverse process syndrome. He was treated by this method. Ashi point was inserted by 1.5 *cun* lateral to the spine. After 3 sessions, he showed complete improvement.

Discussion

The transverse process of L_3 is relatively long, protruding outwards and not covered by sufficient muscles to protect it, so it is easily injured. Puncture and cupping improve *qi* and blood flow in the local area, thus relieving pain.

1.15. Acute Lumbar Muscle Sprain

Acute lumbar pain is a common symptom caused by traumatic sprain of the lumbar region, muscular strain in the lumbar region, or rheumatic myositis of the lumbar muscles. This disease is mostly due to improper posture, falling, wrestling, sprains or contusions which in turn hurts the lumbar muscles, fascias, and ligaments. Its main manifestations are persistent back pain with stiffness of the lumbar spine. Local tenderness may be detected together with limitation of movement of the lumbar spine. One of the two points may be used, Yinjiao (DU 28) or Yaotongdian (EX-UE 7), an extra point.

Point 1
Yinjiao (DU 28)

Location

Yinjiao (DU 28) acupoint is located inside of the upper lip, at the junction of the labial frenum and upper gum (See Fig. 13).

Method

Three-edged needle therapy is used. In most cases of acute lumbar pain, a small vesicle can be detected on the labial frenum about 12 hours after the onset of pain. The vesicle is white or deeply red in color. With the patient in the sitting position, and the neck hyper-extended, raise the upper lip and insert the three-edged needle in the center of the vesicle, then quickly remove it. If excess blood comes out, apply a little white sugar topically. Once the procedure is done accurately, there is no need to repeat.

Result

174 cases were treated by this method. 148 cases were completely cured, 25 cases were improved and 1 case was not

improved. In most cases, the procedure was done once only.

Case

Chui xx, male, 50 years old, worker, with acute lumbar pain after lifting heavy objects. He arrived at the clinic on the second day after the injury occurred. A small vesicle was removed and pain decreased significantly. Diagnosis was acute lumbar muscle sprain. He was treated by this method. On the next day, he had no more pain.

Discussion

1. Yinjiao (DU 28) is interconnected to the Ren Meridian. The Du Meridian controls all Yang meridians, while the Ren Meridian controls all yin meridians. As the Du Meridian is a midline back meridian, it flourishes the back with qi and blood. Hence, removing the vesicle relieves stagnation of qi and blood, thus alleviating lumbar pain.

2. If you do not have a three-edged needle or you cannot use it properly, use a syringe needle to remove the vesicle.

Point 2
Yaotongdian (EX-UE 7)

Location

Two points on the dorsum of each hand, between the 1st and 2nd and between the 3rd and 4th metacarpal bone, and at the midpoint between the dorsal crease of the wrist and metacarpophalangeal joint (See Fig. 14).

Method

Acupuncture is used. Manual stimulation of Yaotongdian

(EX-UE 7) extra points is done in cases of acute lumbar pain, when no vesicle can be found. Use the point on the affected side. Use a 1 *cun* needle of size number 26. Insert the needle 0.3 to 0.4 *cun* deep and stimulate strongly until the patient feels *qi* in the back. Meanwhile, ask the patient to exercise their back muscles.

Result

120 cases were treated by this method. 58 cases were completely cured, 43 cases were much improved, and 19 cases were slightly improved.

Case

Shen xx, male, 17 years old, student. He got a low back injury while playing basketball at school. His initial symptoms were a painful, stiff and hot low back. Viewing the X-ray radiogram, we could see that his bones were intact. Pain was much decreased after his first puncture treatment, and completely relieved after the second visit.

1.16. Chronic Lumbar Muscle Strain

Chronic lumbar muscle strain is caused, when the lumbar muscles are intensely strained in a continuous or repeated way within a short period of time, which exceeds the physiological endurance and, therefore, results in a chronic aseptic inflammation in the lumbar muscular fibers. The occurrence of the illness is closely related with the damp room one lives in or damp ground one lies or sits on. It manifests itself in a long-time pain in the lumbar of one side or both sides, which will be aggravated when the patient is tired, but relieved when he has some gentle activity.

Point

Pigen (EX-B4)

Location

Pigen (EX-B4) extra point is located on the low back, below the spinous process of the 1st lumbar vertebra, 3.5 *cun* lateral to the posterior midline (See Fig. 15).

Method

Acupuncture and moxibustion are used. Select the point on both sides with the patient lying down in the prone position, a 3 *cun* needle is inserted obliquely (with an angle of 45°) to a depth of 2-2.5 *cun* until the patient feels *qi* sensation going down, even to the knee. Apply moxa around the needle until the local area is red with little sweating and retain for 20 minutes, then apply cup to the needle and leave for further 10 minutes. Repeat daily; one course is 8 sessions.

Result

100 cases were treated by this method. 82 cases were completely cured, 11 cases were improved, and 7 cases did not show any effect. All the patients were treated for 1-10 sessions, on the average of 5 sessions.

Case

Zhou xx, male, 56 years old, presented with chronic recurrent low back, pain with limitation of movement and morning stiffness. Plain X-ray showed normal spine. TCM diagnosis is chronic lumbar muscle strain due to stagnation of blood. He was treated by this method. His pain was markedly improved after 10 treatments

Discussion

Chronic lumbar muscle strain, low back pain is mainly due to trauma, wind, cold or damp, all injuries the surround kidney. Kidney Meridian is related to the Extra Meridians. Pigen (EX-B4) point is located in the area of extra meridian. Stimulation of Pigen (EX-B4) point evenly by finger pressure can greatly improve pain.

1.17. Sciatica

Sciatica is a kind of radiating and continuous pain in the course of sciatic nerve distribution, i.e. pain in the hip region, the posterior lateral aspect of the thigh and leg, and lateral aspect of the foot. According to its etiology, sciatica can be divided into the primary and secondary types. The primary type sciatic neuritis is caused mainly by pathological stimulation, pressing or injuring of the adjacent nerves affecting the sciatic nerve. This is also clinically known as symptomatic sciatica. The secondary sciatica is more common than the primary.

Point
Shuangyang (Experience Point)

Location

Draw a straight line between Huantiao (GB 30) and Fengshi (GB 31); from the midpoint of the line, go posterior perpendicularly for 1 *cun*. One *cun* above and one *cun* below the last point are located the two Shuangyang acupoints. The point is between gall bladder and urinary bladder meridians. [N.B: Huantiao (GB 30) point is located at the junction of the lateral 1/3 and medial 2/3 of the distance, between the great trochanter and the hiatus of the sacrum. Locate this point while the patient is in the lateral position with the thigh flexed. Fengshi (GB 31) point is located on the midline on the lateral aspect of the thigh, 7 *cun* above the transverse popliteal crease] (See Fig. 16).

Method

Acupuncture is used. Select Suangyang acupoints on the affected side, and insert a 3 *cun* needle at each point, directed towards each other to a depth of 2.5 *cun*. Manipulated by lifting up and rotating method strongly until the patient feel *qi* sensation going down even to the foot. Then apply moxa until local area becomes red, and retain for 20 minutes. And then apply flash cup and leave for 10 minutes. Repeat daily.

Result

44 cases were treated by this method. 27 were completely cured, 11 were markedly improved, and 2 cases did not show any improvement.

Case

Wang xx, female, 45 years old, farmer, presented with chronic low back and leg pain, accompanied by limitation of movement, and coldness of the leg. TCM diagnosis was sciatica due to cold and damp. After 10 session's treatment, she was completely improved.

Discussion

Sciatica is mainly due to wind, cold and damp, so moxa and

cupping are quite effective methods, Shangyang acupoint related to the roots of sciatic nerve, and the main muscles and vessels around the root. Stimulating this point would much improve sciatic pain, low back pain and leg pain.

1.18. Pain in Lower Back and Leg

Pain in lower back and leg is a common clinic symptom. It is caused by sciatica, lumbar sprain, hyperplasia of lumbar vertebra and prolapse of lumbar intervertebral disc. Its main clinic manifestations are pain from lumbar region radiative to foot, limited movement, which are increased after movement.

Point
Xiashandian (Experience Point)

Location
Xiashandian acupoint is an experience point. Draw a straight line between Zhibian (BL 54) and Huantiao (GB 30). This line is from the base of equal sided triangle with the apex directed posterior in relation to the base. The apex is Xiashandian point (See Fig. 17).

Method
Acupuncture is used. With the patient lying down on the contra lateral side, select the point on the affected side. Use a 3-4 *cun* needle inserted to a depth of 2.5-3.5 *cun*. Manipulate the needle by quick lifting and thrusting until the patient feels *qi* sensation going down to the foot. Repeat daily.

Result

259 cases were treated by this method. All were completely cured, 184 cases needed one session, 61 cases needed two sessions and 14 cases needed three sessions.

Case

Wang xx, male, 30 years old, worker, developed lower back and leg pain on falling down while lifting heave object, with pain and tenderness on the 4th and 5th sacra vertebra. Lumbosacral spine was normal on X-ray. Diagnosis was lumbar sprain. He was treated by this method, and was completely cured after one treatment.

Discussion

Xiashandian (experience point) is also effective for pain and numbness of the thigh. If patient does not feel *qi* sensation, the procedure is of no value. Also avoid cold and exercise during treatment.

1.19. Heel Pain

Painful heel is due to either Achilles tendinitis or pathological conditions of the calcaneum, such as chronic sprain, inflammation, prolapse in calcaneum. It manifests through a painful foot upon walking with tenderness (Ashi points) along the affected side of foot and sole of the foot around and distal to the calcaneum.

Point

Ashi point

Location

This Ashi point is located on the tender spot of the calcaneum.

Methods

1. Massage therapy is used. With the patient lying supine and the leg muscles relaxed, massage is applied for 10 minutes. The technique is to rub and roll the fingers. Repeat daily for 10 sessions.

2. Moxibustion therapy is used. Rub Ashi point with ginger, apply a piece of ginger on the affected area, then ignite moxa cone, put over the ginger. Use 3-5 cones each time. One course is 10 sessions of treatment.

Result

115 cases were treated by this method with moxa and massage. 102 cases were completely cured, 8 cases were improved and 5 cases did not show any effect.

Case

Qian xx, male, 54 years old, presented with pain in right heel, exaggerated on exposure to cold weather, accompanied by coldness and numbness of right foot. His X-ray film showed calcaneum spur. Diagnosis is prolapse of calcaneum. He was treated by both Method 1 and Method 2. He was dramatically improved after two treatments.

1.20. Knee Pain

Besides arthritis, sudden movements such as falls or unexpected pressure may cause lesion to soft tissues such as muscles, tendons, ligaments, etc. Its main manifestations are painful, tenderness swelling and limitation of movement.

Point
Xiyan (EX-LE 5)

Location

Xiyan (EX-LE 5) extra point is located in the depressions on both sides of the patellar ligament when the knee is flexed. The medial and lateral points are named "Neixiyan" and "Waixiyan" respectively (See Fig. 18).

Method

Electric acupuncture is used. Let patient lie down with a pillow beneath the knee to keep it flexed at $120°$. Insert two needles at medial and lateral Xiyan (EX-LE 5) points for a depth of 1.0-1.5 *cun* directed towards the center of the knee until the patient feels *qi* arriving. Connect needles to electric machine with continuous wave frequency until the maximum the patient can bear, and keep for 30 minutes. Repeat everyday or every other day.

Result

146 cases were treated by this method. 120 cases were completely cured, 16 cases were markedly improved, 11 cases were improved and 6 cases had no improvement. The total improvement rate was 95.89%. Most of the patients were improved after the first treatment.

Case

Hu xx, male, 54 years old, farmer, presented with chronic

recurrent knee pain increasing on exposure to cold and accompanied by redness and limitation of knee movement. Diagnosis was arthritis of knee. He was treated by this method. He had much better on the first treatment and had no complaint of joint pain after 8 sessions.

Discussion

1. The exterior Xiyan (EX-LE 5) point pertains to the stomach is the richest in *qi* and blood flow among the 12 regular meridians. On applying the electric machine to medial and lateral Xiyan points the flow of *qi* and blood along the knee is optimally maintained, thus alleviating symptoms.

2. The knee should be flexed at 120° during the procedure to avoid painful insertion of the needle and allow the needle to go smoothly deep to the center of the joint.

1.21. General Pain

General pain refers to any pain in a part of the body or all the body. The pain is due to some diseases, which are developing, such as some chronic painful diseases. If the pain is continuous, the patient will feel tired, insomnia, restlessness and so on.

Point

Ear Apex (MA-H 6)

Location

Ear Apex (MA-H 6) auricular point is located at the top of the helix, opposite to the posterior border of superior antihelix crus (See Fig. 19).

Method

Acupuncture is used. Select the point on both sides, a 1 *cun* needle is inserted to a depth of 0.3-0.5 *cun*. Directed downward and backward. Rotate the needle gently until the patient feels burning sensation in the local area of the ear. Retain the needle for 20-30 minutes, and repeat manipulation every 10 minutes. If the pain recurs in severe cases, you can use retained needles. Retain for 2-3 days then change. One course is 6-8 sessions.

Result

87 cases with different types of pain were treated by this method. 48 cases were completely cured, 34 cases were improved and 25 cases did not respond. Total improvement rate was 94.6%.

Discussion

This method is suitable for headache, sciatica, shoulder and arm pain, low back pain including lumbago, rheumatic and rheumatoid arthritis, rheumatic myositis, intercostal neuralgia, visceral pain, post operative pain, and some cancer cases pain is usually relieved within 5 minutes. This method is four times more potent than any other analgesic.

1.22. Angina Pectoris

Angina pectoris refers to colic pain in heart, caused by chronic coronary insufficiency or acute myocardial ischemia. It generally is from coronary heart disease. Its main manifestations are chest pain radiating to the left back and shoulder or medial side of the left arm. Its sudden onset is often induced by excess fatigue, excessive eating, cold or excitement, and it usually lasts for 3-6 minutes and can be alleviated by rest or medication.

Point
Zhiyang (DU 9)

Location
Zhiyang (DU 9) acupoint is located on the back, and on the posterior midline, in the depression below the spinous process of the 7th thoracic vertebra (See Fig. 20).

Methods
1. Acupressure is used. Let the patient sit down leaning forward. When the angina pectoris occurs, press perpendicularly on the point Zhiyang (DU 9) with the border of a small coin until the pain decreases or vanishes.

2. Intradermal needle therapy is used. A 0.5~1.0 *cun* intradermal needle is inserted at the point Zhiyang (DU 9) and covered with plaster. If the pain recurs, anyone can press with the tip of finger on the point (DU 9), change the needle every 3-4 days. One course is 6-8 sessions. (NB: The pain relief after pressure or retained needle lasts up to 40 minutes).

Results
1. 40 cases were treated by the first method. 39 cases were improved, and 1 case was not improved.

2. 26 cases were treated by the second method. 23 cases were markedly improved, 2 cases were improved and 1 case remained the same.

Discussion
1. Angina pectoris is due to deficiency or stagnation of

Yang *qi* and blood. Du Meridian controls all Yang meridians in the body. Manipulation of Zhiyang (DU 9) acupoint can improve *qi* and blood flow in all Yang meridians.

2. According to the theory of relations between organs, the point Zhiyang (DU 9) is directly behind the heart, Zhiyang (DU 9) point is thus specific for coronary pain.

3. The manipulation at the point Zhiyang (DU 9) means pressing with a piece of coin, and is also diagnostic for coronary pain. If the pain disappears, it is due to coronary heart disease; the reverse is also true.

4. The procedure is simple that it can be done at home, especially if pain recurs frequently. Anything with a pointed tip, e.g., the cover of a cup, can be put on bed with the patient lying down on it so that the cup tip is beneath the point Zhiyang (DU 9).

1.23. Cholecystalgia

Cholecystalgia refers to acute gallbladder pain. It usually caused by acute cholecystitis (acute infection of biliary tract), cholelithiasis (gallstones) or biliary ascariasis. Its main manifestations are severe pain, a kind of paroxysmal colic or a sudden upward drilling pain in right upper abdomen. The pain makes the patient turn from side to side on the bed, cry, nausea, vomiting, sweating or even sufferings from rigidity of the limbs.

Point 1
Root of Auricular Vagus (MA-PS)

Location
Root of Auricular Vagus (MA-PS) point is located corre-

sponding to helix crus, at the root of ear and the juncture between the ear back and mastoid process (See Fig. 19).

Method

Acupuncture is used. With the patient in the sitting position, the doctor stands behind him and pushes the auricle upward to expose the point Root of Auricular Vagus (MA-PS), select the point on both sides. A 1 *cun* needle is inserted for 0.5 *cun* deep and rotated. Retain for 20 minute and rotate every five minutes. Also electric machine with continuous wave frequency current can be applied for 20 minutes.

Result

18 cases were treated by this method, the pain slopped in all cases within 15 minutes.

Case

Wang xx, female, 26 years old, pregnant (seven months). She presented with right hypochondrium pain, accompanies by vomiting and not relieved by anticholinergic drugs. TCM diagnosis is bilitary ascariasis due to heat and damp. She was treated by this method, and after three sessions, the pain had been markedly improved without further need of drugs.

Point 2
Dannang (EX-LE 6)

Location

Danang (EX-LE 6) extra point is located at the tender spot 1-2 *cun* directly below Yanglingquan (GB 34) (See Fig. 21).

Method

Acupuncture is used. Select the point on both sides with the patient in the siting or lying position, a 2 *cun* needle is inserted perpendicularly for 1.5 *cun* deep and rotated until the patient feels *qi* sensation up along the leg and pain decreases. Retain for 20 minutes. If pain recurs, repeat the procedure every 5 minutes.

Result

43 cases were treated by this method. The pain stopped in 28 cases, decreased in intensity in 12 cases, and remained the same in 2 cases.

1.24. Renal Colic

Renal colic is usually caused by urinary calculus (renal stones). Its main clinic manifestations are sudden attacks of paroxysmal lancinating pain. The pain is over the renal region and radiates to the external genitalia and medial aspect of the thigh. The pain, lasting for several minutes or several hours, is accompanied with pale complexion, cold sweating, nausea, or vomiting. Shock may be seen in severe cases. Physical examination reveals percussion tenderness over the kidney region and tenderness at the costovertebral angle.

Point

Yaotongdian (EX-UE 7)

Location

Yaotongdian (EX-UE 7) extra point is located on the dorsum of each hand, with two points between the 1st and 2nd and between the 3rd and 4th metacarpal bone, and at the midpoint between the dorsal crease of the wrist and metacarpophalangeal joint (See Fig. 14).

Method

Acupuncture is used. Select the point on the affected side, a 1 *cun* needle is inserted perpendicularly for 0.5 *cun* deep. Rotate the needle strongly by the reducing method until the patient feels *qi* sensation and pain stops. Retain the needle for 20 minutes. If pain recurs, repeat manipulation every 5-10 minutes.

Result

21 cases were treated by this method, and all had pain relief. 17 cases had relief after 3-5 minutes, 4 cases pain stopped after 5-10 minutes treatment. Two cases came back after 3-6 hours, and procedure was repeated and pain was relieved.

Case

Chen xx, male, 30 years old, who presented with left renal colic and vomiting. X-ray film showed left renal stone. Pain was not relieved by analgetic. He was treated by this method. The pain decreased after the treatment for two minutes and was relieved after 10 minutes.

1.25. Gastrospasm

Gastrospasm belongs to stomach neurosis. It includes pylorospasm and cardiospasm. Their main clinic manifestations are epigastric pain. Pylorospasm is accompanied by severe pain in epigastrium, and cardiospasm is accompanied by pain and vomiting.

Point
Banmen (Experience Point)

Location
Banmen (experience point) is located on the palmar aspect of the hand at the middle of the 1st metacarpal bone, slightly inclined to the ulnar side of palm. Confirm location by local tenderness (See Fig. 22).

Method
Acupuncture is used. Select the point on both sides, a 1.5 cun needle is inserted perpendicularly for 0.5-1.0 cun deep, manipulate strongly with the reducing method until the patient feels qi sensation going up the arm and pain decreases. Retain the need for 20-30 minutes; if pain recurs, repeat manipulation every 5-10 minutes.

Result
30 cases were treated by this method, and pain has markedly decreased in all cases after one treatment.

Case
Shu xx, female, 32 years old, presented with epigastric pain accompanied by restlessness and sweating after exposure to cold. Diagnosis was gastrospasm. She was treated by this method. Pain was relieved within 5 minutes. The needle was further retained for 20 minutes.

1.26. Acute Abdominal Pain
Acute abdominal pain is a common symptom in clinic. It is

caused by internal organs' functional and organic change, such as acute gastritis, acute gastroenteritis, spasm of stomach and intestine, biliary ascariasis, acute cholecystitis, acute pancreatitis, acute appendicitis, acute urocystitis and dysmenorrhea. Clinical manifestation is severe pain in abdomen.

Point 1
Neiguan (PC 6)

Location
Neiguan (PC 6) acupoint is located on the palmar side of the forearm and on the line connecting Quze (PC 3) and Daling (PC 7) acupoints, 2 *cun* above the crease of the wrist, between the tendons of long palmar muscle and radial flexor muscle of the wrist (See Fig. 23).

Method
Acupuncture is used. Let the patient lies down, relax and bend both knees. Select the point Neiguan (PC 6) on bilateral, a 1.5 *cun* needle is inserted deeply towards Waiguan (SJ 5) until you can feel the tip of the needle through the skin on the dorsal (radial) side of the forearm. Let the patient takes a deep breath and ask him/her to hold it. During breath holding rotate the needle and repeat this every five minutes for 20-30 minutes. [Waiguan (SJ 5) acupoint is located 2 *cun* above the transverse crease of dorsum of wrist between the radius and the ulna.]

Result
200 cases were treated by this method. 119 cases had complete remission, 34 cases were markedly improved, 26 cases were partially improved and 21 cases did not respond. In 71 %

of improving cases pain disappeared after 10 minutes.

Case

Gao xx, male, 19 years old, solder, presented with acute abdominal pain, not responding to anticholinergics. Diagnosis was acute bacillary dysentery. He was treated by this method. The pain disappeared after 5 minutes puncture. After 7 sessions pain was completely relieved.

Discussion

Neiguan (PC 6) is one of the five general points, which can be used to treat all types of chest and abdominal pain. The point Neiguan (PC 6) promotes Yang *qi* of all abdominal organs, thus regulating visceral muscle movement.

Point 2
Zusanli (ST 36)

Location

Zusanli (ST 36) acupoint is located on the anterior lateral side of the leg, 3 *cun* below Dubi (ST 35), one finger breadth (middle finger) from the anterior crest of tibia (See Fig. 9).

Method

Acupoint injection is used. Mix 50 mg phenergan with 0.5 mg atrapine in one syringe, inject 1/2 of the amount at each side of the point Zusanli (ST 36), on both sides at a depth of 1.5 cm.

Result

77 cases were treated by this method, and all had pain relief. The duration of manipulation was variable, one minute in 6

cases, 1-5 minutes in 54 cases, 6-10 minutes in 8 cases, 11-20 minutes in 8 cases, and more than 2 minutes in one case.

Discussion

1. This point Zusanli (ST 36) is used for severe case not responding to needling of the point Neiguan (PC 6).

2. Zusanli (ST 36) is controlled by L_5 nerve. L_5 nerve controls visceral muscle movement.

1.27. Toothache

Toothache, a common symptom in stomatopathy, can be due to pulpitis, dental caries and periodentitis, and be aggravated by stimulatoin of either cold or heat. It is more of a complaint of children and the aged with poor body constitution.

Point 1
Yatongling (Experience Point)

Location

Yatongling (experience point) is located on the palmar aspect of hand, between the 3rd and 4th metacarpal bones, about 5 *cun* proximal to the crease between the metacarpal bone and the phalanges. The exact location depends on local tenderness (See Fig. 24).

Method

Acupuncture is used. Select the point on the affected side. A 1 *cun* needle is inserted to a depth of 0.5 *cun* and is rotated by the reducing method until the patient feels *qi* sensation and pain was improved. Retain for 20 minutes. If pain recurs, repeat manipulation every 5 minutes.

Result

112 cases of toothache were all treated for one session. 82 cases had no more pain, 28 cases showed little improvement and 2 cases still had the same pain.

Point 2
Yemen (SJ 2)

Location

Yemen (SJ 2) acupoint is located on the dorsum of the hand, between the 4th and 5th fingers, at the junction of the red and white skin, proximal to the margin of the web (See Fig. 25).

Method

Acupuncture is used. Select the point on the affected side, a 1 *cun* needle is inserted to a depth of 1 *cun*, and is rotated by the reducing method till the patient feels *qi* sensation and pain was improved. Retain for 50 minutes. If pain recurs, repeat manipulation every 5-10 minutes.

Result

385 cases were treated by this method. 303 cases showed marked improvement and 8 cases had no improvement.

Chapter II
Internal Diseases

2.1. Arrhythmia

Any abnormality in the starting portion of heart-stroke, heart rate and rhythm, and cardiac conduction is call arrhythmia, in which tachycardia, bradycardia and irregular heart rate are more common. It belongs to the categories of "palpitation", "severe palpitation" and others in traditional Chinese medicine.

Point
Neiguan (PC 6)

Location
Neiguan (PC 6) acupoint is located on the palmar side of the forearm and on the line connecting Quzi (PC 3) and Daling (PC 7), 2 *cun* above the crease of the wrist, between the tendons of long palmar muscle and radial flexor muscle of the wrist (See Fig. 23).

Method
Acupuncture is used. Use bilateral points, directed towards to Waiguan (SJ 5) for 1-1.5 *cun* deep, use rotating and lifting up and down manipulation, until the patient feels *qi* sensation. In old patient with chronic arrhythmia, use reinforcing method, retain needle for 15-30 minutes. If the patient is young and a

new case, use the reducing method strongly, leave needle for 5 minutes. Repeat daily.

Result

84 cases were treated by this method. 14 cases were completely cured, 20 cases were markedly improved, 44 cases were improved, and 6 cases had no result.

Case

Wang xx, female, 45 years old, after a fight with her family, had arrhythmia, palpitation, and pain in chest, heart rate 180/min, and ECG shown frequent ventricular premature beats. Diagnosis was arrhythmia. Treated by this method, after getting *qi* one minute, breath and heartbeats were abnormal in rate and rhythm.

Discussion

1. The point Neiguan (PC 6) belongs to pericardium meridian; this point is special for heart rate. It functions in two ways: This point can be used to decrease heart rate, if it is quick. If the heart rate is slow, it can be used to regain.

2. The point Waiguan (SJ 5) can be used to support Neiguan (PC 6), with the direction of puncture towards Waiguan (SJ 5).

2.2. Coronary Atherosclerotic Cardiopathy

Coronary Atherosclerotic Cardiopathy, "coronary heart disease" for short, is due to myocardial ischemia resulting from angiostenosis caused by coronary atherosclerosis. The main clinical manifestations are angina pectoris, myocardiac infarction, myocardial sclerosis, etc. The disease pertains to the categories of "obstruction of *qi* in the chest", "angina pectoris", "precordial pain with cold limbs" and others in traditional Chinese medicine.

Point
Neiguan (PC 6)

Location

Neiguan (PC 6) acupoint is located on the palmar side of the forearm and on the line connecting Quzi (PC 3) and Daling (PC 7), 2 *cun* above the crease of the wrist, between the tendons of long palmar muscle and radial flexor muscle of the wrist (See Fig. 23).

Methods

1. Acupuncture is used. Use two 2 *cun* needles at bilateral points, insert 1.5 *cun* towards Weiguan (SJ 5), and rotate quickly for 2 minutes until patient feels *qi* sensation, which should go to elbow, shoulder and heart. If *qi* is local, you would press with your finger along preicardium meridian. This may let *qi* sensation go up. If still no *qi* up to heart, stop for 5 minutes and do it again, this time let needle obliquely towards heart. Once patient gets *qi*, retain the needles 30 minutes. Repeat daily, one course is 10 sessions.

2. Acupressure is used. Patient can do this by himself. Use the tip of thumb press or rub for 10 minutes, 1-2 times daily.

Results

1. 36 cases were treated by the first method. 16 cases were excess type with chest painful, palpitation, and all were completely cured. 20 cases were deficiency type with chest painful only, and 18 cases were completely cured, and 2 cases were of

no result.

2. 20 cases were treated by the second method. After two courses, 18 cases were improved.

Cases

1. Pu xx, female, 35 years old, complained of paroxysmal pain in left chest for 9 days, aggravated 4 days; the pain radiated to left shoulder and back. ECG showed frequent ventricular premature beats. Diagnosis was coronary heart disease. Patient felt severe palpitation, pain and fullness in chest, with pale face. Treated by the first method, she was markedly improved after 20 minutes.

2. Yang xx, male, 51 years old, officer. He had hypertension and coronary disease for many years. ECG showed coronary ischemia. Pain in chest, with pale face, sweating. Treated by the second method for one time, he got better; continued for two courses, he was completely cured.

Discussion

In severe and acute case, use the first method, acupuncture. In mild and chronic case, use the second method, acupressure.

2.3. Hypertension

Hypertension may be divided into two kinds: essential hypertension and secondary hypertension. This section only deals with essential hypertension. It is a chronic, systemic vascular disease characterized by rising of the arterial pressure, especially rising of the diastolic pressure, more than 12.6 kPa (95 mmHg). In the early stage, there are symptoms of dizziness, headache, palpitation, insomnia, tinnitus, dysphoria, lassitude, hypomnesis, etc. In the late stage the organs such as the heart, brain, kidneys and others may be involved. It belongs to the categories of "dizziness" and "headache" in traditional Chinese medicine.

Point
Shenque (RN 8)

Location

Shenque (RN 8) acupoint is located on the middle abdomen and at the center of the umbilicus (See Fig. 26).

Method

Medicated compress is used. Use two kinds of herbs Chuanxiong (Chuanxiong Rhizome, *Rhizoma Ligustici Chuanxiong*) and Wuzhuyu (Evodia Fruit, *Fructus Evodiae*) in equal amounts, ground them together, make a mixture, and mix into a thick paste with vinegar. Fill the navel with the paste and cover the umbilicus with a 4 cm square plaster. Change it after three days. Remove and reapply another; one course is 10 times. Be careful keeping the area dry; do not wash near the plaster.

Result

118 cases were treated by this method. After one month, 77.5% of the patients' blood pressure was improved, and the total effective rats was 82.3%. The method is better at I and II type hypertension.

Case

Wang xx, male, 45 years old, doctor. He felt dizziness and headache for three years; his blood pressure was 21.3/13.3 kPa (160/100 mmHg). ECG was normal. Diagnosis was hypertension (I type). He stopped using all medicines for hypertension, and started using this method. After five days, his blood pressure was normal, and dizziness and headache disappeared.

Discussion

Shenque (RN 8) acupoint belongs to the Ren Meridian. This point is the most special point of all regular points. The herbs can penetrate through umbilicus into blood circulation. The two herbs have indication in hypertension. Therefore this method can be used to treat hypertension.

2.4. Hypotension

Hypotension is one of clinical common symptoms. Normal adult systolic pressure is 12.0-18.7 kPa (90-140 mmHg), and diastolic pressure is 8.0-12.0 kPa (60-90 mmHg). Hypotension refers to systolic pressure less than 12.0 kPa, diastolic pressure less than 8.0 kPa. It is included acute hypotension and chronic hypotension. Acute hypotension manifests coma and shock together in the same time, while chronic hypotension manifests no symptoms or dizziness, giddiness, asthenia, etc.

Point

Xiaergen (MA-PS)

Location

Xiaergen (MA-PS) auricular point is located at the lower most rim of the root of ear (See Fig. 19).

Method

Auricular acupuncture is used. Use press needles or seeds to put at the bilateral points. Press the needle or seeds 2-3 times a day for 15 minutes in each time. After 3-4 days, remove and put a new one. One course is one month.

Result

49 cases were treated by this method. In all cases blood pressure were lower than normal. The cases were completely cured after 3-7 treatments, and the blood pressure became normal.

Case

Zhang xx, male, 60 years old. His blood pressure was 90/60 mmHg for 6 month, accompanied by dizziness, restlessness. Diagnosis was hypotension due to deficiency of *qi* and blood. He was treated by this method, and his blood pressure was 130/85 mmHg after two treatments. Continued for one-month treatment, he was completely cured.

2.5. Common Cold

Common cold is an acute viral or bacterial catarrhal inflammation of the upper respiratory tract. Clinically, it manifests as nasal obstruction, running nose, sneezing, sore throat, hoarse voice, etc. Accompanied with low fever, lassitude, headache, soreness and pain of the limbs, etc.

Point 1
Fengchi (GB 20)

Location

Fengchi (GB 20) acupoint is located on the nape, below the

occipital bone on the level of Fengfu (DU 16), in the depression between the upper ends of sternocleidomastoid and trapezius muscles (See Fig. 1).

Method
Acupuncture is used. Choose bilateral points, use a 1.5 *cun* needle, directed to the tip of nose, insert 1 *cun* deep with reducing manipulation until the patient feels *qi* sensation, and retain the needles for 20 minutes. Once daily for 3-5 days is enough.

Result
50 cases were treated by this method. The total effective rates were 56%, 63.5% and 65% in two, four and six days. The effective rates of headache, cough, running nose and nasal obstruction were 92%, 29%, 70% and 60% respectively.

Case
Zhang xx, male, 50 years old, officer. He had common cold, headache, cough, and running nose. After three treatments, all the symptoms disappeared.

Point 2
Dazhui (DU 14)

Location
Dazhui (DU 14) acupoint is located on the posterior midline, in the depression below the 7th cervical vertebra (See Fig. 20).

Method
Acupuncture and cupping are used. A 1.5 *cun* needle is inserted obliquely toward head for 1 *cun*, by reducing manipula-

tion until the patient feels *qi* in local area, then apply cup for 15 minutes. Once daily for 2-3 days.

Result

73 cases were treated by this method. In most of the cases, one time treatment was needed; some cases needed 2-3 treatments.

Case

Ma xx, male, 26 years old, worker. Because of getting cold and wind after bathing, he felt dizziness, nausea, and vomiting. Check: pale face, sweating, cold in legs and arms, fever, temperature 38℃. After treating by this way, he was better at the same time, and the temperature was normal.

Discussion

1. Du Meridian controls six Yang meridians, and common cold with fever is Yang exceed. The point Dazhui (DU 14) can regulate Yang *qi*.

2. The first point Fengchi (GB 20) can be used to treat common cold without fever and the second point Dazhui (DU 14) with fever.

2.6. Bronchitis

Bronchitis includes acute bronchitis and chronic bronchitis. Acute bronchitis is an acute inflammation of the trachea or bronchi caused by a bacterium, virus, physical or chemical irritation. At the onset, it usually has symptoms of infection of the upper respiratory tract, such as fever, aversion to cold, general aching, etc. Cough is the main symptom. At the beginning it is a nonproductive cough, becomes a productive cough with a little sticky sputum or thin sputum after 1-2 days, gradually, purulent sputum or white and sticky sputum. The course of the disease seldom goes beyond one month. Chronic bronchitis refers to chronic inflammation of the bronchial mucosa and tissues around it. Its etiology is associated with the virus, bacterium, physical or chemical irritation, immune state, vegetable nerve functional disturbance and other factors. Its main clinical manifestations are cough expectoration, or accompanied with dyspnea, etc. The episode of attack lasts at least three months annually for more than two years.

Point
Tiantu (RN 22)

Location

Tiantu (RN 22) acupoint is located on the neck and on the anterior midline, at the center of suprasternal fossa (See Fig. 27).

Methods

1. Acupuncture is used. Patient sits with back and head on a lazy back. Use a 2 *cun* needle, first puncture perpendicularly for 0.2 *cun*, and then insert vertically with the needle tip downward along the posterior aspect of the sternum for 1.5 *cun*. Slightly rotate until patient feels *qi* sensation, distension, heaviness in local area, then remove. Repeat 1-2 times daily.

2. Point injection is used. Patient lies down, putting pillow under neck, use a 5 ml of syringe, take 10% glucose 1 ml, Vitamin B_1 1 ml and Vitamin B_{12} 1 ml, insert obliquely at about $40°$ angle toward down 3-4 cm deep. Until patient feels *qi* sensation in chest, distension and heaviness, push 1/2 the amount. Repeat

every anther day about 4-5 times.

Results

1. 50 cases were treated by the first method. Acute tracheitis usually was completely cured after 1-2 times treatments. Chronic tracheitis usually needs 5-7 treatments for improvement.

2. 800 cases were treated 1-2 times by the second method. 320 cases were completely cured, 400 cases were improved and 80 cases had no effects.

Case

Huang xx, male, 42 years old, complained cough and tracheitis for two years, recurrent every winter, took medicines without effect, with sore throat. X-ray showed increased bronchovascular shadows. After one treatment, his cough was alleviated and after three treatments, he was markedly improved.

Discussion

1. The first method is for acute and new disease, and the second method is for chronic and old disease.

2. The point Tianshu (RN 22) should be used carefully, no more than 2 ml of injection.

2.7. Bronchial Asthma

Bronchial asthma is a bronchial allergic disease with repeated attacks. Different antigens, such as pollen, dust, fish and shrimp, fur, etc usually cause it. Its pathogenical characteristics are bronchospasm, muscle edema, and bronchial obstruction due to hyperscretion. The main clinical manifestation is repeated paroxysmal attacks of dyspnea with wheezing and expiratory dyspnea. The disease belongs to the category of "asthma with wheezing" in traditional Chinese medicine.

Point 1
Danzhong (RN 17)

Location

Danzhong (RN 17) acupoint is located on the chest and on the anterior midline, on the level of the 4th intercostal space, at the midpoint of the line connecting both nipples (See Fig. 26).

Methods

1. Acupuncture is used, use a 2 *cun* needle, insert horizontally direct tip down for 1.5 *cun*. Reducing method with rotating until patient gets *qi* sensation. Retain the needle 30 minutes, once daily for 10 days.

2. Three-edged needle and cupping therapy are used. Sterilize local area around the point with 75%alcohol, use a three-edged needle for little bleeding. Raise and fold skin around the area with left hand, top 1-2 times quickly with right hand, for 2-3 mm, press the area with two hands to let more blood come out, then apply a cup to let more blood out. Retain for 15 minutes. Total amount of blood is 2-3 ml. Repeat every other day for 5 times.

3. Catgut embedding therapy is used. Use surgical needle, pass around the point, the distance is 1 cm from inside to outside, cut the surgical suture bilateral tips and covered by plaster. Leave it for two weeks; no need to repeat.

Results

1. 35 cases were treated by the first method. 19 cases were completely cured, 11 cases were markedly improved, and 14 cases were improved. One case showed no result.

2. 13 cases were treated by the second method. Nine cases were completely cured, and 4 cases were improved.

3. 50 cases were treated by the third method. 35 cases were completely cured, 3 cases were markedly improved, 8 cases were improved, and 4 cases showed no effect.

Cases

1. Ding xx, male, 24 years old, worker. He had asthma for 7 years. The disease increased in winter and anther, happening at any time for 5-7 hours, continue from days to months, difficult breath, full in chest, restlessness, and sweating. He had taken many Western medicines for long time. He was treated by the first method, and after 12 time treatments, was completely cured.

2. Patient, female, 15 years old. She had had a common old since 12 years old. After that, a cough and asthma occured from bad air. She was treated by the second method, and was completely cured after three treatments.

3. Xiong xx, female, 14 years old, student. Since 7 years old she had got common cold, and then lead to asthma. The symptoms increased as she presented. Treated by the third method she was completely cured after one treatment.

Point 2
Dingchuan (EX-B 1)

Location

Dingchuan (EX-B 1) acupoint is located on the back, below

the spinous process of the 7th cervical vertebra, 0.5 *cun* lateral to the posterior midline (See Fig. 28).

Methods

1. Electric acupuncture is used. Use a 1.5 *cun* needle in bilateral, insert 1 *cun* perpendicularly (reducing during attack, reinforcing in between attacks) until the patient gets *qi* sensation in local area and to the front of chest. Use electric machine at a continuous frequency for 20 minutes. Once daily for 10 days.

2. Point injection is used. Use the point at bilateral. 10 mg verapamil are divided for 5mg in each point, insert about 1.5 *cun*. Repeat every other day; one course is 10 treatments.

Results

1. 197 cases were treated by the first method. All the cases were treated 1-2 courses. Completely cured in 105 cases, markedly improved in 64 cases, improved in 28 cases.

2. 40 cases were treated by the second method. After 2-9 times treatment, 15 cases were completely cured, 12 cases were markedly improved, 6 cases were improved, 7 cases were of not effect. The total effective rate was 82.5%.

Cases

1. Zhang xx, male, 53 years old, officer, had asthma for more than 10 years. In the past 3 years, attacked by common cold every time for about two months. He was treated by the second method, and after 3 times of injection, completely cured for 12 years.

2. Gou xx, male, 14 years old, student, had extrinsic asthma after common cold for 3 years, getting severe. After two treatments by the first method, asthma stopped for one year.

Discussion

It is better to use the point Dingchuan (EX-U 14) during attack. Use Tanzhong (RN 17) in between attacks. Also you can use both points at the same time.

2.8. Hiccup

Hiccup is the cramp of diaphragm often seen after an abdominal operation or the later stage of a serious disease. A normal person may also have hiccup from gulping too much or having uncooked cold food.

Point
Yifeng (SJ 17)

Location

Yifeng (SJ 17) acupoint is located posterior to the ear lobe, in the depression between the mastoid process and mandibular angle (See Fig. 3).

Methods

1. Acupressure is used. Patient sits down, with doctor behind the patient. Use the tip of both index fingers to press on both Yifeng (SJ 17) points, directed from one point to other at the same time. Patient takes deepest inhalation, and holds it as much as possible. If hiccup does not stop, after the first time, repeat another 2-3 treatments.

2. Acupuncture is used. The method is the same as the first one, but use needles, for the depth of 1 *cun* and insert rotating once until patient gets *qi* sensation, and then retain for 30 minutes.

Results

1. 32 mild cases were treated by the first method. 18 cases stopped after first treatment, 6 cases stopped after second treatment, 5 cases after third treatment, and 3 cases after fourth treatment.

2. 126 severe cases were treated by the second method. 106 cases were completely cured, and 20 cases were of no result.

Cases

1. Liu xx, male, 21 years old. He often had hiccup after eating, and could not sleep. He used his index fingers to press the point and always got an improvement.

2. Wang xx, male, 29 years old. Continuous hiccup for 3 days, increased after eating, poor sleep. Took Western medicines without effect. Treated by the second method, he got completely cured after 3 treatments.

Discussion

1. It is better to use the first method for mild and acute case, and the second method for severe and chronic.

2. The first method can be used to treat hiccup by patient himself/herself or his/her relatives at home.

3. Deep breathing during treatment is very important.

2.9. Chronic Gastritis

Chronic gastritis is a nonspecific inflammation of gastric mucosa. It may be divided into the superficial, atrophic and hypertrophic according to its pathogenic changes. The main clinical manifestations are epigastric pain, indigestion, anorexia, etc. The disease pertains to the category of "epigastric pain" in traditional Chinese medicine.

Point
Zhongwan (RN 12)

Location
Zhongwan (RN 12) acupoint is located on the up abdomen and on the anterior midline, 4 *cun* above the center of umbilicus (See Fig. 26).

Method
Acupuncture and moxibustion are used. Use a 2 *cun* needle, insert perpendicularly for 1.5 *cun* in depth, thrust and rotate by reinforcing method. Once patient feels *qi* sensation around epigastrium, apply moxa stick to put on the handle of the needle, ignite it, and use three sticks. Repeat daily for up to 10 days.

Result
154 cases were treated by this method. 151 cases with chronic gastritis were improved, 3 cases chronic gastritis accompanied by cancer or ulcer, showed no effect. The total effective rate was 98.1%.

Case
Wang xx, male, 58 years old. Complained pain in epigastrium for 10 years. Aggravated since six months ago, poor appetite, losing weight. Examination by X-ray showed gastritis. Treated by this method, alleviated after seven treatments, he had good appetite, and then continued for seven times in every other day, with markedly improvement.

Discussion

1. It is necessary to apply a paper with a small hole in the center, put it on the local area before moxibustion, so that the moxa stick won't hurt skin.

2. This method is better for treating chronic stomach pain due to deficiency cold type.

2.10. Vomiting

Vomiting is a condition referring to the casting up of food substance or gastric fluid from the stomach through the mouth. Vomiting may be seen in many diseases, such as acute or chronic gastritis, cardiospasm, phylorospasm, cholecystitis, pancreatitis and gastroneurosis.

Point
Zhitu (Experience Point)

Location

Zhitu (experience point) is located on the palmar aspect, 0.5 *cun* below the middle of the main wrist crease (See Fig. 23).

Method

Acupuncture is used. A 1 *cun* needle at bilateral point, insert obliquely toward the tip of middle finger, at an angle of 15°-30° for 0.8 *cun*, and rotate by reducing method. Until patient feels *qi* sensation (numbness, distension, in middle finger or hand), retain needle for 30 minutes. If vomiting is not stopped, repeat the manipulation every 5 minutes.

Result

26 cases were treated by this method. In most of cases vomiting stopped after one treatment; in some cases it needs two treatments. Vomiting stopped in 21 cases after one treatment, in 5 cases after two treatments. It did not recur in 22 cases.

Case

Zhang xx, female, one year old, had vomiting and diarrhea for two days. She vomited 20 times and diarrhea 10 times at night, had fever and poor appetite, without eating and drinking anything. Treated by this method for two treatments, stimulating strongly and quickly, vomiting and diarrhea was stopped.

2.11. Diarrhea

Diarrhea is manifested by increased defecation with watery loose or mucoid stools, often seen in acute or chronic enteritis, intestinal tuberculosis, intestinal dysfunction and irritable colon, etc.

Point

Diarrhea Point (Experience Point)

Location

Draw a straight line from the center of exterior malleolus to planta, the place at which it meets the border of red and white line of sole is Diarrhea Point (See Fig. 29).

Methods

1. Moxibustion is used. Use bilateral point, ignite moxa stick, 1 *cun* away from the point, every side for 15 minutes. Re-

peat 1-2 times daily; one course is 10 days.

2. Acupuncture is used. Use bilateral point, 1 *cun* needle insert perpendicularly 0.8 *cun*. Reducing method until patient feels *qi* sensation around local area, retain 20 minutes. Repeat daily for 5 day. If diarrhea is severe, you can use electric machine.

Results

1. 120 cases were treated by the first method. 18 cases were completely cured, 2 cases were improved, and 50 cases were treated one time, 59 cases were treated two times, 7 cases were treated three times.

2. 40 cases were treated by the second method. The rate of complete cure was 85%, markedly improved was 7.5%, improved was 5%, and no effect was 2.5%.

Cases

1. Lin xx, male, 6 months baby, had indigestion for long time, diarrhea 10 times daily; stools showed watery with white flocculent and smelled rancid; restlessness, crying, poor sleep. Treated by the first method, and moxibustion two times, the baby had good sleep, diarrhea alleviated. After the third treatment, all symptoms disappeared and he was completely cured.

2. Zhuo xx, male, 42 years old, complained diarrhea due to cold drinking and eating, 4-5 times in one night, loose watery, accompanied by pain in abdomen, intestinal gurgling sound, tender around umbilicus. Diagnosis was acute diarrhea. Treated by the second method, it was stopped after one treatment.

Discussion

The first method, moxibustion, is suitable for child and chronic diarrhea; the second method, acupuncture, is for adults and acute diarrhea.

2.12. Constipation

Constipation is a condition manifested by prolonged intervals of dry or compacted feces from the intestines, or urgent desire for immediate bowel movement but with difficulty on defecating. It commonly includes habitual constipation, constipation due to peristalsis dysfunction and constipation due to rectum or anus disorders in Western medicine.

Point 1
Tianshu (ST 25)

Location

Tianshu (ST 25) acupoint is located on the middle abdomen, 2 *cun* lateral to the center of the umbilicus (See Fig. 30).

Methods

1. Acupressure is used. Patient lies down, bending knees to relax abdomen muscle. Use the tips of index finger to press the bilateral points Tianshu (ST 25) for 10 minutes. Repeat it everyday. It is better do it in the morning before getting up; one course is seven days.

2. Electric acupuncture is used. Patient lies down. Use 3 *cun* needles at bilateral points, when patient feels *qi* sensation. Connecting electric machine with continuous wave for 30 minutes. Repeat it everyday.

Result

8 cases were treated by the second method, electric acupuncture. Generally, on the second day, the patient can defecate. After 7 days, conform good habit in stools.

Case

Zhang xx, male, 30 years old, complained constipation for one year. He took many medicines without result, so was treated by the second method, and was completely cured after 5 treatments.

Point 2
Large Intestine (MA-SC4)

Location

Large intestine (MA-SC4) auricular point is located in the superior concha, anterior and superior to the helix crus (See Fig. 19).

Method

Auricular acupuncture is used. Apply press needles on bilateral points, covered with plaster. Press 3 times, 50 presses for each time in each day; the pressure should be as strong as the patient can bear. Change new needles every three days.

Result

80 cases were treated by this method. Completely cured were 72 cases, 8 cases were of no good result, and needling was done on the average five treatments.

Case

Liu xx, female. 44 years old, complained constipation for 17 years, defecation one time in every 4-5 days. Diagnosis was habitual constipation. Treated by this method, for five days the stool was soft; after 10 days, she was completely cured.

2.13. Retention of Urine

Retention of urine refers to difficult urination resulting in large amounts of urine accumulated in the blabber, clinically characterized by blockage of urine and distension and fullness in the lower abdomen.

Point

Liniao (Experience Point)

Location

Liniao (experience point) is located midway between Qugu (RN 2) and Shenque (RN 8), and it is not Ren Meridian point (See Fig. 31).

Methods

1. Acupressure is used. Use the tip of thumb, starting slowly and gently, to press and roll at the acupoint for 15 minutes until the patient feels desire to pass urine, and continue until finishing urination.

2. Acupuncture is used. Use a 1.5 *cun* needle to insert for 1 *cun*. Rotating method will be used, until patient feels *qi* sensation around local area and feels urination sensation. If not, keep needle repeating the manipulation after 5 minutes, until passing urine.

Result

44 cases were treated by this ways and 40 cases got good result.

Case

Shun xx, male, 15 years old, student. He had difficult urination after taking tranquilizer. He felt distension in lower abdomen, restlessness. Diagnosis was retention of urine. He was treated by the second method, and passed urine 300 ml after 30 seconds. His urine was normal after 2 hours.

Discussion

1. All the points between Qugu (RN 2) and Shenque (RN 8) are located in Ren Meridian, which can be used to treated retention of urine, but the best point is the midway one, Linia (experience point) which we are using.

2. It is important first to choose acupressure. If not effective, needle will be used.

3. It is better that patient do acupressure by himself at home, after treatment in clinic.

2.14. Urinary Incontinence

Urinary incontinence refers to involuntary urinary discharge when patient is conscious of it. It is mostly seen in elderly patients, female patients or patients who have survived a traumatic experience. The urine drips spontaneously without control.

Point

Ciliao (BL 32)

Location

Ciliao (BL 32) acupoint is located on the sacrum, medial and inferior to the posteriosuperior iliac spine, just at the 2nd posterior sacral foramen (See Fig. 32).

Methods

1. Acupuncture is used. A 2 *cun* needle is used bilateral to the point, inserted 1.5 *cun* deep with reinforcing manipulation for deficiency type and reducing for excess type, until the patient feels *qi* sensation in the lower abdomen, connect electric machine with a pulse wave for 30 minutes. Repeat daily.

2. Point injection is used. Use 2ml of vitamin B_1 and 1ml of 0.9% saline, inject 1.5 ml for each point in 2cm deep. Repeat every other day. One course is five treatments.

Results

1. 18 cases were treated by the first method. After 3-6 treatments 10 cases were completely cured, 7 cases were improved, and 1 cases was not effective.

2. 50 cases were treated by the second method. After 3-6 treatments, 37 cases were completely cured with an effective rate of 74%, 7 cases were improved with an effective rate of 14%, and 6 cases showed no effect taking 12%.

Cases

1. Jiang xx, female, 36 years old. She had had urgency of urination, frequency of micturition for one year, and manifested involuntary discontinuous urination for six month. She was treated by the first method and got markedly improved after one treatment. She was completely cured after 3 treatments.

2. Zhu xx, female, 3 years old. She had lower intelligence

quotient, could not speak, and had involuntary urination and stools. She was treated by many medicines and long needling but had no effect. Diagnosis was urinary incontinence. Treating by the second method, after nine treatments, she can control urine and stools, and also her intelligence got better.

Discussion

1. The first method is for mild cases, and the second method is for severe cases.

2. It is very important to insert the needle at the depression exactly.

2.15. Impotence

Impotence refers to the weakness of penis erection during sexual intercourse, characterized by poor erection that lasts only for seconds. For impotence as a main symptom due to sexual neurasthenia or some other chronic diseases, the differentiation and treatment in this section can be referred to.

Point

   Guanyuan (RN 4)

Location

Guanyuan (RN 4) acupoint is located on the anterior midline, 3 *cun* below the umbilicus (See Fig. 31).

Methods

1. Acupuncture and moxibustion are used. Use a 3 *cun* needle, insert 2-2.5 *cun* deep. With reinforcing method until the patient feels *qi* sensation, directed to penis. Apply moxa stick

(1.5cm) up to 3 cones. Repeat daily for up to 3 times.

2. Catgut embedding therapy is used. Sterilize local area with 75% alcohol, use surgical needle and 00# catgut suture, pass around the point from up to down, the distance from inside to outside is 1cm, cut the suture bilateral and cover it by plaster, leave of two weeks. Do not need repeat.

Results

1. 12 cases were treated by the first method. After 1-4 treatments, 7 cases were completely cured, 3 cases were markedly improved, and two cases were improved.

2. 31 cases were treated by the second method. After 1-2 treatments, 28 cases were completely cored and 3 cases were improved.

Cases

1. Wang xx, male, 29 years old, officer. He was impotence for six month. From starting, he had a hard penis, but it led to impotence. Diagnosis was sexual neurasthenia. He was markedly improved after 2 treatments.

2. Chen xx, male, 42 years old, officer. He was impotence for 3 years. He took many medicines without effect. Examination showed that his genitourinary was normal. Diagnosis was sexual neurasthenia. He was treated by the second method, improved after one treatment.

Discussion

If patient does not like to go to doctor, he can use moxa at home every day for 30 minutes before sleep.

2.16. Seminal Emission

Seminal emission refers to the involuntary seminal discharge that takes place often apart from during sexual intercourse. Specifically, nocturnal emission happens during dreams in sleep while spermawtorrhea happens when the patient has no dreams or completely clear during sleep, However, occasional seminal emission in adult males, married or unmarried, is not considered as a disease. For seminal emission caused by prostatitis, neurasthenia, seminal vesiculitis and other diseases in Western medicine, the differentiation and treatment this section can be referred to.

Point
Zhongji (RN 3)

Location

Zhongji (RN 3) acupoint is located on the anterior midline, 4 *cun* below the umbilicus (See Fig. 31).

Method

Acupuncture and moxibustion are used. Use a 3 *cun* needle, insert 2-2.5 *cun* deep. With reinforcing method until the patient feels *qi* sensation, directed to the penis. Apply moxa stick (1.5cm) up to 3 cones. Repeat daily for up to 3 times.

Result

14 cases were treated by this method. 12 cases were completely improved, 1 case was improved, and 1 case had no effect.

Case

Zheng xx, male, 23 years old, worker. He had seminal emission 1-2 times in every night for six months. He had felt headache, pain in lower back for more than one year. Diagnosis was seminal emission due to deficiency of kidney Yin. He was treated by this way and got completely cured after 11 treatments. He now has normal sexual life after one year.

2.17. Facial Paralysis

Facial paralysis refers to peripheral facial paralysis caused by an acute nonsuppurative inflammation of the facial nerve in the stylomastoid foramen. Clinic manifestations are sudden onset, sluggishness, numbness of the face and paralysis of the affected side, deviation of the angle of the mouth to the healthy side, with incomplete closure of the eye, and the nasolabial groove becomes shallow.

Point
Yifeng (ST 17)

Location
Yifeng (SJ 17) acupoint is located posterior to the ear lobe, in the depression between the mastoid process and mandibular angle (See Fig. 3).

Methods
1. Acupuncture is used. Select a 1.5 *cun* needle, insert affected side point, in the direction to another ear, with 1 *cun* deep, (manipulation reducing for acute case, reinforcing for chronic case) until the patient feels *qi* sensation in local area by rotating method, retain the needle 30 minutes. Repeat daily. After needling, use cupping therapy. Apply quick flash cupping, each

time for five minutes. One course is ten times.

2. Point injection is used. Use Vitamin B_1 2ml and Vitamin B_{12} 1 ml inject affected side of facial paralysis; use 1.5 ml of the mixed liquid, inject at depth of 1 cm directed toward other ear. Repeat every other day.

Results

1. 32 cases were treated by the first method. After 3 courses, 31 cases were cured, 1 case showed no result. Most of the cases were treated 1-2 course.

2. 60 cases were treated by the second method. 48 cases were completely cured, 11 cases were improved and 1 case showed no effect in two courses.

Cases

1. Ding xx, male, 26 years old, complained that he suddenly could not drink water nor could close his right eye in one morning. He went to doctor and was found to have mouth change to left side, and loss of forehead crease. TCM diagnosis was facial paralysis due to wind and cold. He was treated by the first method and was improved after one treatment. He was completely cured after ten treatments.

2. Zhang xx, female, 53 years old, worker. She had had left facial paralysis for two years, numbness in left face, muscle to it spasm, deviation of the angle of the mouth to the right. She went to many doctors, with no effect. Diagnosis was left facial paralysis. She was treated by the second method. After 3 treatments, she could open her mouth and drink water normally; after four treatments, she was completely cured.

Discussion

The first method, acupuncture, can be used in new cases. The second method, point injection, can be used in standing cases.

2.18. Facial Spasm

Facial spasm, more common in women over middle age, refers to spasm on one side of the face in irregular attacks. Clinical manifestations initially include only intermittent spasms of the orbicular muscles. Gradually, the spasm involves other muscles of the face. There will be convulsions of the mouth corner in the severe case. Fatigue, mental stress or physical movement may aggravate the severity of the convulsions or spasm. Convulsions spontaneously stop during sleep. Some patients may also have headache and tinnitus. Neurological system examinations show positive signs.

Point
Houxi (SI 3)

Location

Houxi (SI 3) acupoint is located at the junction of the red and white skin along the ulnar border of the hand, at the ulnar end of the distal palmar crease, proximal to the 5th metacarpophalangeal joint when a loose fist is made (See Fig. 7).

Method

Acupuncture is used. Patient is in sitting position. Choose affected side point. Use a 1.5 *cun* needle, insert 1 *cun* deep, directed towards to Hegu (LI 4). Apply reducing technique with rotating and thrusting, until patient feels *qi* sensation. Continue the manipulation every five minutes, until patient cannot bear. Repeat daily. One course is three sessions.

Result

8 cases were treated by this method. 1 case was completely cured after one treatment, 4 cases were improved after three treatments, and 3 cases were improved after five treatments.

Case

Liu xx, female, 32 years old, attendant. She complained of right side facial tic for 15 days, and paroxysmal right facial muscle spasm continued about one hour. Diagnosis was facial tic. After being treated by this method, the spasm stopped in 30 seconds, and the patient felt better. The needle retained for 30 minutes. The patient was completely cured with just one treatment.

2.19. Cerebrovascular Accidental Sequela

Cerebrovascular accidental sequela refers to hemiplegia, slurred speech, deviation of the mouth and eye, urinary incontinence and other symptoms caused by acute cerebrovascular diseases, pertaining to the category of "wind stroke" in traditional Chinese medicine. Here we deal with hemiplegia, aphasia, and urinary incontinence due to cerebrovascular accident.

1) Hemiplagia due to Cerebrovscular Accident

Point
Baibui (DU 20)

Location

Baihui (DU 20) acupoint is located on the head, 5 *cun* directly above the midpoint of the anterior hairline, at the midpoint of the line connecting the apexes of both ears (See Fig. 4).

Method

Acupuncture is used. Use a 1.5-2 *cun* needle on affected side. Insert horizontally under skin for 1-1.5 *cun* deep, directed to the point Qubin (GB 7); insert continually three sections between the two points Baihui (DU 20) and Qubin (GB 7). Rotate the needle quickly at a frequency of 200 times per minute, continuing for 5 minutes and stopping for 5 minutes. Repeat three times about 30 minutes, and then remove the needles. Once daily; 15 treatments are in one course.

Result

500 cases were treated by this method. After 1-3 courses, 478 cases were improved, and 22 cases had no change.

Case

Sun xx, female, 56 years old, worker. She suffered cerebral thrombosis for 14 days, treated by Western medicine with some improvement, but she was unable to move the affected side. She came to the acupuncture treatment. 16 hours later after the first treatment, she could walk about 20 meters with support. After the second treatment, she could walk alone. Her arm and hand could move after three treatments.

2) Aphasia due to Cerebrovscular Accident

Point
Yumen (Experience Point)

Location
Yumen (experience point) is located on the midline of the back of tongue, 1 *cun* from the tip of tongue (See Fig. 33).

Method
Acupuncture is used. Patient sits or lies down, with his/her mouth open. Doctor holds the tongue out with the left hand, uses a 2 *cun* needle in the right hand, inserts horizontally to 1.5 *cun* deep, and directed toward the root of tongue, use even technique until patient feels throat hot and can say "Ah---". Treat once daily; one course is of six treatments. Rest 3-5 days between two courses.

Result
75 cases were treated by this method, and all the cases were improved.

3) Urinary Incontinence due to Cerebrovascular Accident

Point
Tongtian (BL 7)

Location
Tongtian (BL 7) acupoint is located on the head, 4 *cun* directly above the midpoint of the anterior hairline and 1.5 *cun* lateral to the midline (See Fig. 4).

Method

Acupuncture is used. Select a 1.5-2 *cun* needle, insert horizontally for 1-1.5 *cun* at bilateral points, directed toward the point Luoque (BL 8), rotate quickly (200 times per minutes), continue three minutes, rest for 5 minutes, and then continue for three minutes again. The whole treatment takes about 30 minutes.

Result

30 cases were treated by this method. After 3-10 times treatment, 15 cases were completely cured, 10 cases were markedly improved, 3 cases were improved, and 2 cases had no effect.

Case

Li xx, female, 65 years old, complained headache, dizziness for one month, sudden hemiplegia, aphasia, urinary and bowel incontrollable, leading to coma. Blood pressure: 26.7/16.0 kPa (200/120 mmHg), CT diagnosis was left cerebral hemorrhage, treated by Western medicine with some improvement, but persistent urinary incontinence. Treated by this method one time, she could feel urination; after three treatments, she could control urination.

2.20. Rheumatic Chorea

Rheumatic chorea refers to involuntary movements, accompanied by disturbance of voluntary movement, muscle weakness and emotional, characterize rheumatic chorea, also known as minor chorea. It is mostly seen in children, but more often in women adults. It is mainly caused by rheumatic fever, however, factors like scarlet fever, diphtheria, encephalitis, hypothyroidism, etc. may also give rise to rheumatic chorea.

Point
The Chorea-Trembling Controlled Area

Location
The chorea-trembling controlled area: the parallel line is located 1.5 *cun* in front of the motor area (See Fig. 34).

Method
Acupuncture is used. Patient is in sitting position. Use a 1.5 *cun* needle, insert 1 *cun* deep, rotating at an angle of 30°. Rotate the needle at a frequency of about 150-200 times per minute, continue for 3 minutes and stop for 2 minutes, then continue for 3 minutes again. Three times in each session. Repeat daily, one course is ten days. Rest for 2-3 days between two courses.

Result
20 cases were treated by this method: 5-10 years old patients (13 cases), 10-20 years old patients (7 cases). After one course treatment, 14 cases were completely cured, 5 cases were improved and 1 case showed no effect.

Case
Ding xx, male, 16 years old, student. He complained of pressure in eyes, flash in front of eyes for two months. In the past 5 days, his mouth and right hand had involuntary movements, and head involuntary shook to right and left. Examination: conscious, no problem in speaking, cerebration and eyes are normal. Diagnosis was rheumatic chorea. After one treatment, he could control the moving of mouth and right hand; af-

ter five treatments, he could control all movements; after 10 treatments, he was completely cured.

2.21. Spasmodic Tortocouis

Spasmodic tortocouis refers to cervical muscle paroxysmal and involuntary contraction leading to deviation of head or clonic obliquity to one side. Clinical manifestations are cervical muscle spasm and rigidity involuntary leading to head to one side, aggrieved by nervous, disappearing during sleep.

Point
Binao (LI 14)

Location
Binao (LI 14) acupoint is located on the lateral side of the arm, at the insertion of deltoid muscle and on the line connecting Quchi (LI 11) and Jiaoyu (LI 15), 7 *cun* above Quchi (LI 11) (See Fig. 35).

Method
Acupuncture is used. Patient is in sitting position. Choose bilateral point. Use a 2 *cun* needle, insert obliquely 1.5 *cun* deep directed downward (toward hand), and apply reducing technique until patient feels *qi* sensation to hand. Retain the needle for 30 minutes.

Result
4 cases were treated by this method, and all were improved.

Case

Liang xx, male, 40 years old, farmer, had sudden torticollis two months earlier. He had muscle spasm in right neck, and deviation of head to right side with an angle of 45°, retaining 3-5 seconds for each time and 30 minutes between two spasms, consciousness, no spasm during sleep. Diagnosis was spasmodic torticollis. He was treated by this method for 4 times and was cured. He had recurrence a year later, and was treated by the same method for two times and completely cured with no recurrence.

2.22. Numbness of Hand

Numbness of hand is generally caused by cervical spondylopathy leading to numbness or pain in fingers, hand and arm, finger rigidity or difficult movement, and decreased slip strength. Symptoms are lateral or bilateral. Some cases are accompanied by dizziness, nausea, blurry vision, etc.

Point
Jingbi (Experience Point)

Location

Jingbi (experience point) is located above the upper border of clavical of internal 1/3 and external 2/3, external border of steinomastoid muscle (See Fig. 36).

Method

Acupressure is used. Patient sits down, and doctor stands in front of him. Choose the point on the affected side, left hand fixes patient's shoulder, tip of thumb of another hand

presses and rolls on the point, first gently, then gradually
stronger until patient feels electric sensation going down to
affected hand. Manipulate about 15 minutes. Repeat daily for
2-3 times.

Result

200 cases were treated by this method, for ten days or years.
Of cases of numbness for days or years, most had 1-2 treatments,
and were improved with no recurrence.

2.23. Systremma

Systremma, also called spasm of gastrocnemius muscle,
refers to sudden colic spasm in lateral or bilateral gastrocnemius
muscle. It is usually caused by cold. Clinical manifestations are
pain in lower leg, difficult movement, paroxysmal spasm, and
alleviated by warmth.

Point

Chengshan (BL 57)

Location

Chengshan (BL 57) acupoint is located on the posterior
midline of the leg, between Weizhong (BL 40) and Kunlun (BL
60), in a pointed depression formed below the gastrocnemius
muscle belly when the leg is stretched or the heel is lifted (See
Fig. 8).

Methods

1. Acupuncture is used. Patient lies in the prone position.
Use the point on affected side, insert a 3 *cun* needle perpen-

dicularly to 1.5-2 *cun* deep with reducing method until the patient feels *qi* sensation around local area. Retain the needle for 30 minutes, and repeat manipulation every 10 minutes.

2. Moxibustion with warming needle therapy is used. Patient lies in the prone position. Choose affected side point, a 2-3 *cun* needle is inserted perpendicularly for 1.5-2 *cun* deep. Put moxa cone on the handle of the needle to ignite it. Repeat 2-3 times with moxa cones; treat daily.

3. Point injection is used. Use the point on affected side, inject 3 ml mixed liquids of 2 ml Vitamin B_1 and 1 ml Vitamin B_{12}, to a depth of 2 cm.

Results

1. 23 cases were treated by the first method. 80% of cases were completely cured in one session.

2. 9 cases were treated by the second method. After 1-3 treatments, 7 cases were completely cured, and 2 cases were improved.

3. 30 cases were treated by the third method. In most of the cases, symptoms alleviated after one treatment, and improved or cured after 2-3 treatments.

Case

Lui xx, male, 65 years old, had bilateral systremma for five years. Symptom was aggrieved by cold, paroxysmal spasm 2-3 times in night. Diagnosis was systremma. Treated by the first method for three times. He was completely cured, with no recurrence in one year.

Discussion

The fist method is used only on first presentient spasm and

pain, it is better in later or chronic spasm to use the second method or the third method.

2.24. Epilepsy

Epilepsy is defined as paroxysmal and temporary disturbance of brain characterized by loss of consciousness and muscle tic or abnormal sensation, emotion or behavior. Clinical manifestations of the disease vary greatly. There may be grand mal, petit mal, rolandic mal and infantile spasms. The grand mal is characterized by sudden loss of consciousness, general spasm with apnea, cyanosis and foam in the mouth, which usually last for 1-5 minutes. The patient may then fall into sleep and become conscious a few hours later. The petit mal is characterized by sudden, short loss of consciousness without aurae and muscle tic, accompanied with interruptions of speech and action which usually persist for 2-10 seconds. The patient usually comes to consciousness rapidly.

Point
   Dazhui (DU 14)

Location
   Dazhui (DU 14) acupoint is located on the posterior midline, in the depression below the 7th cervical vertebra (See Fig. 20).

Method
   Acupuncture is used. Patient sits down bending neck. Use a 1.5 *cun* needle, insert obliquely 1.0 *cun* deep upward. Once patient feels electric sensation to arms, remove the needle (dived insertion no manipulation). Repeat daily or every other day. One

course is 10 times. Rest seven days between two courses.

Result

95 cases were treated by this method. 24 cases were markedly improved (frequency and duration of epilepsy decrease), 45 cases were improved, and 26 cases showed no result.

Case

Zheng xx, female, 12 years old, student, had epilepsy due to head injury since five years old. Present aggravate, epilepsy 1-2 times daily. Took Western medicine dilantin, no result. Half year earlier, the frequency of epilepsy increased. Electroencephalogram was disordered and abnormal; diagnosis was epilepsy. She was treated by this method for seven times. The frequency of epilepsy decreased, once a week, for the duration of five minutes. After 25 treatments, the frequency decreased, once four weeks, for the duration of two minutes. After 35 treatments, it did not occur again; electroencephalogram was normal. Stop all the medicines. In five years, she became normal.

Discussion

Don't manipulate too strong and insert too deep, avoiding hurting marrow. This point regulates any qi in six Yang meridians, thus regulating brain.

2.25. Vertigo

Vertigo, also called dizziness, is the general term for blurred vision and vertigo. The former refers to visionary sparkling or the blurring of vision with darkness appearing in front of the eyes. The later refers to a subjective feeling that the body or surrounding objects are turning around with difficulty to keep balance. They are always mentioned together since both may appear at the same time. Mild dizziness may be stopped by instant closing of the eyes. In the severe case, the patient feels as if he/she is on a fast-moving train or sailing boat that makes him/her unable to stand firmly. Episodes may be accompanied by nausea, vomiting, sweating or fainting in more severe condition. Dizziness may be seen in many cases in Western medicine such as auditory vertigo, cerebral arteriosclerosis, hypertension, vertebrobasilar ischemia, anemia, neurasthenia and those cerebral conditions with dizziness as the main symptom. For the above mentioned conditions, the differentiation and treatment in this section can be refers to.

Point
Baihui (DU 20)

Location
Baihui (DU 20) acupoint is located on the head, 5 *cun* directly above the midpoint of the anterior hairline, at the midpoint of the line connecting the apexes of both ears (See Fig. 4).

Methods
1. Acupuncture is used. Patient is in the sitting position. Insert a 1.5 *cun* needle at Baihui (DU 20), directed toward Shishenchong (EX-4), first to anterior, then left, and then right, finally to posterior, until the patient feels *qi* sensation in each line. Don't go by needle outside skin. Rotating in every line, patient feels heave in head. Then retain the needle for 24 hours.

2. Moxibustion is used. Moxa cone with ginger. Patient is in the sitting position. Remove hair in local area as a coin around

the point Baihui (DU 20). Rub with ginger, put a piece of ginger of 0.3 cm in thickness, punch several holes on it with a needle and place it on the point selected and then put a moxa cone on the ginger, and ignite the moxa cone until the local area skin becomes flush and wet. In general, each treatment needs 7-10 units of moxa cones, once a day. One course is 10 days.

Result

22 cases were treated by the first method. 18 cases were completely cured, 2 cases were improved, and 2 cases had no result. In average there were about 10 times of treatment.

Case

Kong xx, female, 52 years old, worker, had right side hemiplegia for three years and left side hemiplegia for one year, dizziness, insomnia, difficulty in speaking, numbness in arm, and difficulty in movement of the hand. Diagnosis was vertigo due to deficiency of *qi* and blood. Treated by the second method. After one treatment, she felt head and eye clear; after 10 times of treatment, she was completely cured.

Discussion

The two methods can be used in different types. In the first method, acupuncture is used in excess types, and in the second method, moxibustion is used in deficiency types. Baihui (DU 20) is a point at which 12 meridians meet together. Vertigo is due to cold and Yang *qi* deficiency (deficiency type) or stagnation (excess type); the point Baihui (DU 20) may improve cold, Yang *qi* and stagnation.

2.26. Schizophrenia

Schizophrenia is the most common psychosis. Its etiology has not been well understood despite many years of studies. Generally, genetic and environmental factors are considered, which are involved in causing the disease. Schizophrenia frequently occurs in young adults. The ratio of incidence between males and females is roughly equal. It characterized mainly by incoherence of thinking, apathy, delusion, hallucination and etc. It belongs to the category of "manic-depressive psychosis" in traditional Chinese medicine.

Point

Fengfu (DU 16)

Location

Fengfu (DU 16) acupoint is located 1 *cun* directly above the midpoint of the posterior hairline, directly below the external occipital protuberance, in the depression between m. trapezius of both sides (See Fig. 32).

Method

Acupuncture is used. Use a 1.5 *cun* needle, puncture perpendicularly toward the tip of nose for 1 *cun*, according to the type of disease, choose reinforcing or reducing manipulation, even stimulation. The doctor does not need to thrust too hard. It is enough when patient feels the *qi* sensation, remove the needle. Once daily, and 10 treatments are in one course.

Result

10 cases were treated by this method. After 1-2 courses, all of the cases were improved in symptoms.

Case

Patient, male, 26 years old, complained of metal disorder for 4 months, emotional depression, apathy, dementia, divagation and muttering to oneself, frequent crying or laugh for no apparent reason, caprice, no desire for diet, white greasy coating of the tongue, taut and slippery pulse. Diagnosis was schizophrenia. He was treated by this method for six times, and all symptoms were improved.

2.27. Hysteria

Hysteria is a common type of neuroses, occurring more often in young women. The disease is characterized by delusion of grandeur, mannerism, sensitive to hint, etc. Attacks of this disease are often due to mental factors. Here it deals with psychonosema (mental disorder), aphasia and paralysis due to hysteria.

1) Psychonosema due to Hysteria

Point
Renying (ST 9)

Location

Renying (ST 9) acupoint is located on the neck, beside the laryngeal protuberance and on the anterior border of sternocleidomastoid muscle, where the pulsation of common carotid artery is palpable (See Fig. 10).

Method

Acupuncture is used. Patient lies down on the back. Put small pillow under shoulder and expose all neck. Using bilateral point, a 1 *cun* needle is inserted slowly about 0.3-0.5 *cun* in depth, until the patient feels *qi* sensation as numbness, distension and soreness, and the handle of the needles undulating. Retain the needle for 30 minutes. According to different cases, electric machine may be used, and at same time suggestion are given to help the effect.

Result

148 cases were treated by this method. All of the cases got good results in one treatment. Mental state was in order, speaking became normal and all were recovered.

Case

Patient, female, 30 years old, suddenly had uncontrollable movement in legs and arms, difficulty in speaking, and mental disorder. Treated by this way. After 10 minutes, she could walk and speak with high voice, and all the symptoms disappeared.

2) Aphasia due to Hysteria

Point
Lianquan (RN 23)

Location

Lianquan (RN 23) acupoint is located on the neck and on the anterior midline, above the laryngeal protuberance, in the depression above the upper border of hyoid bone (See Fig. 27).

Method

Acupuncture is used. Patient sits down with back and head on a lazy back, and raises his head. Use a 2 *cun* needle, insert obliquely toward up for 1.5 *cun*. When the patient feels strong *qi* sensation soreness and distension, take out the needle under skin, and then, change direction to Jinjin (EX-HN 12) on the left and Yuye (EX-HN 13) on the right, insert 1 *cun* in depth with rotating method. At the same time, the doctor needs to give language suggestion, training speaking, to say "Ah----", "Ba----" or "one, two----". The treatment should be repeated every day or every other day.

Result

30 cases were treated by this method. All were completely cured. 18 cases were in five treatments, seven cases were in 12 treatments and 5 cases were in more than 13 treatments.

3) Paralysis due to Hysteria

Point

Huantiao (GB 30)

Location

Huantiao (GB 30) acupoint is located on the lateral side of the thigh, at the junction of middle third and lateral third of the line connecting the prominence of the great trochanter and the sacral hiatus when the patient is in a lateral recumbent position with the thigh flexed (See Fig. 37).

Method

Acupuncture is used. Patient lies down with lateral side, use a 3 *cun* needle, insert perpendicularly toward genitals for 2.5 *cun* in depth, rotating and lifting by reducing method until the patient feels sensation down to the feet on the same side, and then, treat the other side. Once daily.

Result

41 cases were treated by this method. All cases were improved after one treatment.

2.28. Insomnia

Insomnia is a condition that makes the patient unable to acquire normal hours of sleep. It is usually accompanied by dizziness, headache, palpitation and poor memory. However, insomnia does present different clinical manifestations. In the mild cases, they may be difficult to fall into sleep. Dream-disturbed sleep often wakes up the patient with frightening or makes him unable to fall into sleep again. In severe cases, there can often be no sleep for the whole night.

Point

Zudigenbu (Experience Point)

Location

Zudigenbu (experience point) is located on 2 lines, one from the center of interior malleolus to the center of exterior malleolus, another from middle toe to heel, at which the two lines cross each other in the point (See Fig. 38).

Method

Acupuncture is used. Use bilateral points. A 1 *cun* needle is inserted for 0.5-0.8 *cun* with even rotating method for 1-2 minutes. Retain the needle for 30 minutes or more. Repeat daily. One course is six times.

Result

77 cases were treated by this method. In 1-4 courses, 60 cases were markedly improved (sleeping for 7-8 hours in night, all symptoms disappeared); 15 cases were improved (sleeping extended, symptoms decrease); 2 cases showed no result.

Case

Liao xx, male, 28 years old, officer, had palpitation, insomnia for two years, difficult sleeping until midnight, dizziness, and asthenia tired. He felt better after one treatment by this method. Continue treating for one course, and completely cured.

Chapter III
Surgical Diseases

3.1. Chronic Cholecystitis

Chronic cholecystitis is a common surgical disease. Recurrent episodes of cholecystitis are usually associated with gallstones (more than 90%). The attacks are often less severe than classical acute cholecystitis, and may resemble peptic ulceration and peptic oesophagitis. Myocardial ischaemia may be confused with the side of greatest pain.

Point
Shenque (RN 8)

Location
Shenque (RN 8) acupoint is located on the middle abdomen and at the center of the umbilicus (See Fig. 26).

Method
Moxibustion is used. Patient lies down, use moxa stick 1-2 *cun* above umbilicus around umbilicus until local area is very warm (as much as the patient can bear) for 20 minutes daily.

Result
21 cases were treated by this method. 15 cases were completely cured, four cases were improved and two cases showed

no effect.

Case

Guan xx, male, 45 years old, doctor. The patient had chronic cholecystitis and gallstones for many years. He felt distention in abdomen, nausea, pain in epigastrium radiated to right shoulder. He took Atropine, with no effect. There was more pain on the second day. Diagnosis is cholecystitis. He was treated by this method, and the pain was decreased after two minutes of treatment; five minutes later pain disappearance.

Discussion

The smoke of burning moxa contains volatile oils that can flow through skin to warm meridian.

3.2. Cholelithiasis

Cholelithiasis is a common surgical disease. This disease is caused and affected by cholecystitis and inflammation, and stones are usually found at the same time, so the clinical manifestations are similar to each other. Most stones produce no symptoms, but they may cause: flatulence, biliary colic, acute cholecystitis, chronic cholecystitis, obstructive jaundice, which may be intermittent giving attacks of fever, jaundice and upper abdominal pain. Gallbladder empyema from bile duct obstruction is uncommon.

Point

Danshu (BL 19)

Location

Danshu (BL19) acupoint is located on the back, below the

spinous process of the 11th thoracic vertebra, 1.5 *cun* lateral to the posterior midline (See Fig. 32).

Method

Acupuncture is used. Patient lies down on stomach. Choose points on bilateral, insert a 1.5 *cun* needle for the depth of 1 *cun* obliquely towards midline, reducing manipulation. Once the patient feels *qi* sensation in local area, apply electric machine continuous frequency wave with strong stimulating; retain the needles for 40 minutes. Repeat daily.

Result

50 cases were treated by this method. 40 cases were completely cured, nine cases were improved, and one case showed no effect.

Case

Zhuo xx, female, 46 years old. She had gallstones for 5 month, pain in epigastrium, paroxysmal colic towards right shoulder, vomiting with indigestive food, cold and fever, poor appetite. Check: temperature 39℃, right epigastrium tender. Diagnosis is cholecystitis. She had one treatment by this method, and on the second day pain decreased. Found stones 0.5g in stools. After the third treatment, one stone 3.6×2×1 cm in size, 5.1g in weight, was found in stools. She was completely cured after 6 treatments.

3.3. Biliary Ascariasis

Biliary ascariasis refers to a kind of paroxysmal colic or a sudden upward drilling pain in the upper abdomen due to upward movement of ascarid in the intestine running into the biliary duct. The pain makes the patient turn from side to side on the bed, cry, feel nausea, vomit, sweat or even suffer from rigidity of the limbs, hence the name ascarid colic. The pain can soon be relieved and the patient becomes normal when the ascarid withdraws from the biliary duct.

Point
Yingxiang (LI 20)

Location
Yingxiang (LI 20) acupoint is located in the nasolabial groove, at the level of the midpoint of the lateral border of ala nasi (See Fig. 5).

Method
Acupuncture is used. Patient lies down. Inserted a 1 *cun* needle 0.5 cm perpendicularly, and then change direction up toward the point Sibai (ST 2), insert horizontally with reducing method, cut handle and put plaster covering, leave for 24 hours. Do not repeat.

Result
22 cases were treated by this method. In 13 cases pain stopped, 5 cases have ascarids in stools, 6 patients were improved, and 3 cases showed no change.

Discussion
The point Yingxiang (LI 20) belongs to Large Intestine Meridian, and goes to Stomach Meridian, linking two meridians to make the muscle of gallbladder relax. These can decrease pres-

sure and thus the ascarid is gone.

3.4. Volvulus

Volvulus refers to rotate a section of the intestine. Most of which is occurred in small intestine and lead to intestinal obstruction. It is characterized by abdominal pain, vomiting, abdominal distention, flatulence and difficult bowel evacuation due to impeded intestinal transportation caused by stagnation and obstruction of intestines.

Point

Zhangmen (LR 13)

Location

Zhangmen (LR 13) acupoint is located on the lateral side of the abdomen, below the free end of the 11th rib (See Fig. 39).

Method

Acupuncture is used. Patient lies down. Use the points bilateral, insert horizontally 1 *cun* needles to 0.5 *cun* inside, in the direction to midline with reducing method, patient feels distension, numbness sensation in local area, use electric machine at a continuous frequency wave, with strong stimulation, retain the needles for 20-60 minutes. 1-2 times daily.

Result

114 cases were treated by this method. 102 cases were completely cured (pass stools), 12 cases had no result and needed surgery. Most of the cases got the result after the treatment of 30-60 minutes.

Case

Song xx, male, 24 years old, worker, started to work after eating, suddenly felt pain in abdomen, with vomiting, distension, no gas, no stools, big abdomen, intestinal ansa is around umbilicus. Diagnosis is volvulus. He was treated by this method, and could pass gases after seven minutes, with pain and distention decreased. On the second day, he was completely cured.

Discussion
This point is also used for enteroparalysis post operation.

3.5. Acute Mastadenitis
Acute mastadenitis is an acute suppurative inflammation of the mammary gland. It is caused by the infection of bacteria that invades the breast after the splitting of the nipple or the retention of milk, often seen in breast feeding women and most common in primiparae since it is likely to happen 3-4 weeks after childbirth.

Point
Jianjing (GB 21)

Location
Jianjing (GB 21) acupoint is located on the shoulder, directly above the nipple, at the midpoint of the line connecting Dazhui (DU 14) and the acromion, at the highest point of the shoulder (See Fig. 40).

Method
Acupuncture is used. Patient sits down. Use affected side point, , insert a 1 cun needle perpendicularly for 0.5-0.8 cun,

with reducing method, rotating until patient feels numbness and distension sensation to shoulder and elbow, manipulate for 5-10 minutes, then remove the needle. Two times daily until patient gets better.

Result

393 cases were treated by this method. 390 cases were completely cured (320 cases of 393 had 1-3 treatments, 50 cases of them had 3-7 treatments, 13 cases of them had 7-15 treatments, one case had more than 15 treatment), 3 cases had no result,

Case

Yu xx, female, married, farmer, who complained distension and swollen in breast for 5 days, accompanied by chill, fever, headache, temperature 38.9℃. Her left breast was red with distension; the tumescence was 8×9 cm in size, painful and refused pressing. Diagnosis was acute mastadenitis. Treated by this method, she got better after two treatments, with temperature of 36.7℃, swollen breast and pain decreased. Continue for another two treatments, and she was completely cured.

Discussion

The point Jinjing (GB 21) belongs to Shaoyaong Meridian of Foot, and cross with Yangming of foot and Yanwei meridians, which have close relation to breast, so the point can decrease fire inside breast, reducing stagnation of blood, to treat mastadenitis.

3.6. Ureterolithiasis

Ureterolithiasis, or urinary calxulus is a common disease in the urinary system, including calculus of the kidney, ureteral calculus, vesical calculus and urethral calxulus. This disease incidence appears obviously in certain areas.

Point
Taixi (KI 3)

Location
Taixi (KI 3) acupoint is located in the depression between the tip of the medial malleolus and Achilles' tendon (See Fig. 41).

Method
Acupuncture is used. Patient lies down. Use the point bilateral, insert 1 *cun* needles 0.5 *cun* deep, with the direction toward point Kunlun (BL 60), use reducing method and strong stimulation, until the patient feels numbness and distension in feet, retain the needle for 30-90 minutes. Once daily.

Result
23 cases were treated by this method. After 1-3 treatments, in 18 cases pain disappeared in local area (in 6 cases stones were passed in urine), 5 cases were improved.

Case
Yan xx, male, 54 years old, felt pain in left lumbar region and colic in left lower abdomen, with nausea, vomiting, frequent micturition, urgency of urination. Check: pale, markedly tender in left lower abdomen, blood cells 10-15 in urine; X-ray showed one stone 0.8×0.6 cm in size. Diagnosis is left urethral stone. Treated by this method. Insert needle, the pain decreased after one minute, and then pain disappear; next day he was treated

again, and was completely cured.

3.7. Chronic Prostatitis

Chronic prostatitis is a very common disease of the urinary system in young and middle-aged male patients. The disease is usually a secondary infection of acute prostatitis or posterior urethritis. Sometimes, it may also be a secondary infection of the upper respiratory tract or mouth cavity. The common pathogens are staphylococcus, streptococcus, colibacillus, etc. It is often induced by excessive alcoholic drinking, injury of the perineum, excessive sexual intercourses.

Point

Shenque (RN 8)

Location

Shenque (RN 8) acupoint is located on the center of the umbilicus (See Fig. 26).

Method

Medicated compress therapy is used. Patient lies down. Choose herbs Musk (Moschus) 0.15g and white pepper 7.0g, mixed to make powder, clean the umbilicus with 75% alcohol, put the mixing powder one spoonful to umbilicus, cover it with cotton then plaster, change after seven days. One course is four times; it usually needs six courses.

Result

11 cases were treated by this method. All of the cases had long history about three months to six years. Six cases were completely cured, three cases were improved, and two cases showed no result.

Case

Huang xx, male, 50 years old, officer, felt hot and pain in prineum, difficult to urinate, pain in urethra. Check: swollen prostate and press pain. Diagnosis is chronic prostatitis. He was treated by this method for three courses. Symptoms disappeared, and everything was normal.

3.8. Hemorrhoid

Hemorrhoid refers to swollen or twisted veins in the anus and lower rectum. Generally, all small fleshy prominances that are found at the internal and external areas of the anus are called hemorrhoid, also known as pile or hemorrhoidal lump. This is a common, frequently encountered disease. According to the different location, hemorrhoids can be divided into internal, external and mixed types of hemorrhoids among which the internal type is most common. This disease can cause anus pain, sinking and distending sensation, itching, and bleeding.

Point

Erbai (EX-UE 2)

Location

Erbai (EX-UE 2) extra point is located on the palmar side of each forearm, 4 *cun* proximal to the crease of the wrist, on each side of the tendon of radial flexor muscle of the wrist. Two points (See Fig. 42).

Method

Acupuncture is used. Use the point at bilateral. Take a 1.5

cun needle to insert for 1 *cun* in new or young case with reducing method, and in old or chronic case with reinforcing method, until the patient feels *qi* sensation around local area, repeat every 5 minutes by rotating for 3 minutes, retain the needle for 30 minutes. Once daily, and one course is two weeks.

Result

99 cases were treated by this method. 64 cases were completely cured, 35 cases were improved. 36% of the cases were improved in one week treatment, 19% of cases improved in four weeks treatment.

Case

Tan xx, male, 62 years old, worker. He had mixed hemorrhoid for 21 years, had taken three operations, felt pain and had blood during stools. Diagnosis was hemorrhoid. He was treated for four weeks, completely cured, and had no problems for 10 years.

Discussion

This point Erbai (EX-UE 2) extra point is near lung and pericardium meridian. When puncturing close to Sanjiao Meridian, the three meridians can regulate movement of large intestine, to treat hemorrhiod.

3.9. Eczema

Eczema is a kind of common allergic inflammatory dermatosis. It is divided into acute and chronic types. Acute eczema is characterized by sudden onset of symmetric and polymorphic lesions in repeated attacks, and accompanied by erythma, edema, papule, vesiculation, oozing and intense itching. When cured, it presents decrustation without any traces. The chronic type eczema is transformed from the acute one and characterized by roughness of skin, dark red or gray color of skin in the affected areas, scaled skin or lichen-like skin. Chronic eczema may often bring about acute attacks.

Point
Antihelix (Auricular Point)

Location
Antihelix (auricular point) is located in the center of the antihelix (See Fig. 19).

Method
Cutting therapy is used. Firstly sterilize with alcohol in local area of ear, and then fix the ear with left hand and take operation knife (or three aged needle) with right hand, cut perpendicularly the line of horizontal antihelix (the line is 0.2-0.4 cm in long, 0.1-0.2 cm in deep, to let bleeding 2-3 drops). Apply cotton plaster for 4 hours and release; twice weekly.

Result
12 cases were treated by this method. All of the cases were completely cured after 3-4 treatments, with an average 7 treating days.

Case
Ding xx, female, 18 years old, had bilateral contralateral red papule on external lower legs for 15 days, accompany by vesica, exudation, erosion. On the right side the size was about 8×10

cm, and on the left side it was about 6×8 cm, with border unclear, local skin reddens, severe pain and itching. TCM diagnosis was eczema due to damp and heat of spleen and stomach. Treated by this method for 5 days, she was cured, and the color and sensation of local area are normal.

Discussion

1. If there is no sharp knife, three-aged needle could be used.

2. If patient does not like bleeding, the bilateral ear antihelix retained needle can be used, and press every day for three times for each one, 50-100 presses in per time, three treatments daily.

3. To get more rapid effect in local area, use three egad needle to let a little bleeding.

3.10. Urticaria

Urticaria is a kind of allergic skin disease with skin wheals as the main manifestation. The clinical manifestations are the appearance of wheals over the skin with sudden onset and rapid disappearance, leaving no trace after recovery. There is a sensation of severe itching and burning heat on the affected part. Urticaria can attack repeatedly and last for a long time.

Point
Shenque (RN 8)

Location

Shenque (RN 8) acupoint is located on the center of the umbilicus (See Fig. 26).

Method

Cupping therapy is used. Use big size cup, put it on umbilicus three minutes, then take off, and put it again after three minutes. This is one time. One treatment needs three times. Repeat 2-3 treatments every day.

Result

105 cases were treated by this method. Generally, the patient gets improved about itching and rash after one treatment. Completely cured should be after 3-4 days. The effective rate is 96.19%.

Case

Lin xx, male, 45 years old, officer. He had itching and rash all over the body, particularly on the back. Diagnosis was urticaria due to wind and heat. He was treated by this method. The itching and rash were decreased after two treatments. He got completely cured after another treatment.

Discussion

Urticaria is due to deficiency of immunity. Stimulation umbilicus can increase function of immunity of the body.

3.11. Cutaneous Pruritus

Cutaneous pruritus is a kind of dermatosis, which has a sensation of self-conscious itching on the affected part. It has no primary skin lesion, and belongs to functional disorder of cutaneous sensory nerve. The clinical manifestations are serious paroxysmal itching on the skin, usually occurs at night or as a result of irritating food or emotional upset. It is difficult for the patient to bear and stop the itching while it attacks. Once the itching has stopped, the patient will have any further symptom.

Point
Xuehai (SP 10)

Location
Xuehai (SP 10) acupoint is located, when the knee is flexed, 2 *cun* above the mediosuperior border of the patella, on the bulge of the medial portion of m. quadriceps femoris. Or when the patient's knee is flexed, cup your right palm to his left knee, with the thumb on the medial side and with the other four fingers directed proximally, and the thumb forming an angle of 45° with the index finger. The point is where the tip of your thumb rests (See Fig. 43).

Method
Acupuncture is used. Choose bilateral point. Use 1.5 *cun* needles, insert 1 *cun* with reducing method for excess type, and reinforcing method for deficient type, retain the needles for 30 minutes. Once daily, and one course is 10 treatments. Good result is after three courses.

Result
30 cases were treated by this method. All of the cases were treated for 4-30 treatments. 19 cases were completely cured, 9 cases were improved and 2 cases show no effect. The total effective rate was 93.3%.

Case

Zhu xx, female, 54 years old, officer, felt all body itching for one year. Found papule, scratch mark, on trunk and arms. She felt severe itching, no systemic disorder. Diagnosis was body itching. She was treated by this method. After five treatments, no more itching; after 15 treatments, completely cured.

3.12. Psoriasis

Psoriasis is a kind of chronic erythroderma desquamativum. Its clinical characteristics include erythematous scaly lesion and serious itching. This disease is chronic and can recur. It mostly occurs in young or middle-aged people.

Point
Ear Apex (EP-K 12)

Location
Ear Apex (EP-K 12) auricular point is located at the upper tip auricle and superior to helix when folded towards tragus (See Fig. 19).

Method
Acupuncture is used. Firstly, use a three-aged needle to let bleeding at the point, and then, use a 1 *cun* needle insert horizontally helix for 0.5-0.8 *cun* deep, rotating and repeating for many times, in 30 minutes. One time daily or every other, until completely cured.

Result
50 cases were treated by this method. 32 cases were completely cured, 16 cases were improved, and two cases had no

effect.
Case
Zhang xx, male, 15 years old, student.   Three month earlier he had two or three red, small papule on forehead, itching. After 2-3 days, silvery white squame took off, itching, with no pain, developed until covered 30% of the body. Diagnosis was psoriasis. Treated by this method for 10 times, the squame started taking off and no more new ones appeared. Continued for 5 treatments, all of the papule disappeared, markedly improved.

3.13. Acne
Acne is a chronic inflammation of hair-follicle and sebaceous glands. It often occurs among boys and girls in adolescence. It is called adolescent acne. Its clinical characteristics manifest as papulae, nodules and acnes on the face.

Point
Dazhui (DU 14)

Location
Dazhui (DU 14) acupoint is located below the spinous process of the seventh cervical vertebra, approximately at the level of the shoulders. (See Fig. 20).

Method
Three-edged needle and cupping therapy are used. Patient sits down with arms on the table, use a three-edges needle to tap for 1-2 times for 2-3 mm deep, squeeze to let blood out, then apply cup for 15 minutes (about 2-3 ml blood out), take off the cup. Repeat every other day, and one course is 4 treatments.

Result

39 cases were treated by this method. 29 cases were completely cured, seven cases were improved, and three cases had no change.

Case

Zhang xx, female, 20 years old, student. She had acne for 4 years, and many red papulae on face, particular on forehead; took many medicines, with no result. Diagnosis was acne. Treated one time, no more any new ones appeared; continued for 10 treatments, all the papulae was gone, but just had deep color on the face; after three months' treament, she was completely cured.

3.14. Vitiligo

Vitiligo is an acquired skin disease of localized pigment loss, which is characterized by irregular white patches on the skin without subjective symptom.

Point

Local area

Location

Local area refers to the center of the affect area.

Method

Moxibustion is used. Cup a piece of paper with a small hole, which is of the affected area size in the center. Apply moxa stick to local area; using moxa close to local area until it turns red in color and patient can not bear the pain any more. After 30 treatments, an improvement is obtained. This disease usually happens to many parts on the body. You may choose some for treatment, and then treat others, one by one, until the color changes to normal.

Result

Six cases were treated by this method. All of the cases were completely cured with an average of 25-38 treatments.

Cases

Li xx, male, 42 years old, officer, who had two white patches on his left forehead about 3 cm in diameter for three years. Diagnosis was viteligo. He was treated by this method for 28 times, and was completely cured.

Chapter IV
Obstetrical, Gynecological and Pediatric Diseases

4.1. Dysfunctional Uterine Bleeding

Dysfunctional uterine bleeding is a common gynecological disease. It is an abnormal uterine bleeding caused by ovarian dysfunction. Its clinical manifestations are disorder of menstrual cycle, prolonged and heavy bleeding.

Point
Duanhong (Experience Point)

Location
Duanhong (experience point) is located between the knuckles of the second and middle finger (See Fig. 44).

Method
Acupuncture and moxibustion are used. Do both acupuncture and moxibustion on the point Duanhong (experience point) bilaterally, after sterilizing with 75% alcohol. Choose needles that are between 1.5 to 2 *cun* long. Insert horizontally about one or two *cun* deep. Manipulate with the reinforcing method. When the patient feels *qi*, a slight surging sensation of energy, stop manipulating the needle, and let it remain untouched for 20 minutes. During this time, use the moxa stick in a circular motion

119

around the point, for 10-15 minutes. Repeat this treatment once a day. Ten treatments constitute one course.

Result

Usually one course of this treatment can regulate the menstruation. If the patient has not improved after the first course of treatment, pause for three days, and then begin a second course.

Case

Wang xx, female, 33 years of age, had had continual bleeding for more than one month. The quality of her menstruation was thin; the amount was sometimes profuse and sometimes scanty; the color was light. She used Western medicine to stop bleeding for 13 days, with no effect. Now she felt dizziness, weakness, was always tired, lassitude; she had a sallow complexion; her lips were pale. Traditional Chinese Medicine "beng lou" diagnosed her as having dysfunctional uterine bleeding due to spleen deficiency. One hour after this treatment, interval bleeding had decreased. After the second treatment, the patient experienced no dysfunctional uterine bleeding. Nevertheless, one complete course was recommended to reinforce the treatment, so that it did not re-occur.

Discussion

This method is suitable to treat dysfunctional uterine bleeding due to spleen deficiency. The best result occurs when the patient feels a warm *qi* sensation from the knuckle to elbow, or preferably the shoulder. The point Duanhong has the special function of stopping bleeding, especially in the uterus. It can link all meridians. When *qi* circulation is good, it can control blood, so the blood stays inside the meridian, without leaking out when it is not supposed to.

4.2. Dysmenorrhea

Dysmenorrhea means that women have periodic pain during or prior to or after menstrual period in the lower abdomen or even faint in severe cases. It has been customary to classify cases of dysmenorrhea into two main groups: primary or functional dysmenorrhea referring to the one which is not caused by organic diseases, and secondary dysmenorrhea referring to the one caused by organic diseases in reproductive system.

Point
Shiqizhui (EX-B 8)

Location
Shiqizhui (EX-B 8), extra point is located below the spinous process of the fifth lumbar vertebra (See Fig. 15).

Method
Acupuncture and moxibustion are used. The patient lies in the prone position. Take the point below Lumbar 5, swab with alcohol, use needles 2-2.5 *cun* long. Insert needles perpendicularly about two cun. When the patient feels the *qi* sensation around the local area, quickly rotate the needle to strongly stimulate the patient until the sensation travels to the lower abdomen. Continue manipulating the needle one to two minutes, until the pain decreases and stops. If the patient does not feel better, use the warming needle method. Leave the needle untouched for 20 minutes, if no moxibustion is used, and 10 minutes if the warming needle method is used.

Result

64 cases were treated by this method; 59 cases of which were completely cured; very good results in four additional cases; one case had no effect.

Case

Liu xx, female, 17 years of age, a student. Her first menstruation came at 17 years old, with severe twisting pain in the lower abdomen. She also felt nausea and vomiting, soreness in the low back. Her abdominal pain continued for two hours. Miss Liu's TCM diagnoses was dysmenorrhea due to stagnation of *qi* and blood. By using this method of treatment, pain is decreased in one minute; after three minutes, the patient feels no more pain.

Discussion

This point, Shiqizhui (EX-B 8), is located in the lumbar region. It is located in the Du Meridian. The Du Meridian controls all the Yang of the body; it is the sea of the Yang Meridian. Shiqizhui (EX-B 8) has the function to regulate all the Yang *qi* in the Yang Meridian. Regulating all the Yang meridians make the Yang *qi* circulation in the body good, so there is no more stagnation, and pain is stopped. From a Western viewpoint, this point is on a nerve and relates to the nervous system, so it can regulate the uterine muscle. Pressing on the point can stimulate the nervous system, to make the muscle relax, and relieve spasms felt from muscle contraction.

4.3. Leukorrhagia

Leukorrhagia means morbid leukrrhea, which is a disease

symptomized by persistent excessive mucous vaginal discharge. It refers to profuse leukorrhea with abnormal color, quality and smell, accompanied with constitutional or local symptoms.

Point

Sihua (Experience Point)

Location

Sihua (experience point) is located on the back. These four points make the shape of a flower 1.5 *cun* on either side of the spinal column, just below T7 and T10 (See Fig. 45).

Method

Acupuncture is used with the patient lying prone. Use 1.5 *cun* needles and insert them obliquely to the mid-line about 1.0 *cun* deep. If the leukorrhea is yellow or red, use the reducing method. If the leukorrhea is clear or white, with dizziness, palpitation or low back pain, use the reinforcing method. When the patient feels a *qi* sensation, leave the needles for 20 minutes. A patient with a deficiency syndrome may need 40 minutes or more with the needles. Treatments should be given once a day. Treatment can be done whether the woman has her period or not; the length of treatments depends upon the response of the woman.

Result

28 cases were treated by this method, 20 of which had white, six had yellow, and two had red leukorrhea; after being treated from one to six times, 21 cases were completely cured, and six cases improved; one case had no change. The average treatment was three or four times.

Case

Yuan xx, female, 25 years of age, married. She had had leukorrhagia for six months, felt dizziness, palpitation, hunger, tired, and weak. The TCM diagnosis was leukorrhagia due to spleen *qi* deficiency. After three treatments, her leukorrhea ceased, but she still had dizziness, palpitation, hunger, was tired and weak. After another week without treatment, the patient's remaining symptoms were gone as well.

4.4. Sterility

Primary sterility refers to married women, who live together with their spouse and have normal sexual relations for over two years, and fail to be pregnant without contraception. Secondary sterility refers to those women who fail to be pregnant over two years after having a previous delivery, miscarriage, or abortion, without contraception.

Point

Guanyuan (RN 4)

Location

Guanyuan (RN 4) acupoint is located on the anterior midline, 3 *cun* below the umbilicus (See Fig. 31).

Method

Moxibustion is used. Indirect moxibustion with ginger is used on Guanyuan (RN 4). The ginger should be about 2 cm in diameter and 2~3 mm in thickness. Prick holes in the ginger, before placing a big moxa cone on top. Five cones are used per treatment twice daily, morning and evening before sleep. Ten treatments are one course. Usually one to five courses is needed. No treatments should be done during the woman's menstruation.

Result

30 cases, married more than two years, without children, were treated by this method; after five courses of treatment, 11 of these women had a child in the first year; treatments were stopped after five courses.

Case

Wang xx, female, 24 years of age. After four years of marriage, she had no child. She always was depressed, felt cold, tired, and had no appetite. Western medicine diagnosed her as having twisted fallopian tubes and wanted to do an operation. She refused and went to get a Traditional Chinese Medicine diagnosis and treatment. TCM diagnosed her as having kidney *qi* and Yang deficiency. After five courses of moxibustion, she got pregnant. Eight months later, she had a baby.

Discussion

The point Guanyuan (RN 4) belongs to the Ren Meridian, and has a relationship to the Du and Chong meridians. It is the origin of all three of these meridians. Moxibustion on this point can warm and stimulate them. The Chong, Du and Ren meridians control gynecological function.

4.5. Chronic Pelvic Inflammation

Pelvic inflammation is an inflammation occurring in the internal genital organs (including uterus, fallopian tubes and ovaries), pelvic connective tissues and pelvic peritoneum. Clinically, it is further divided into acute pelvic inflammation and chronic pelvic inflammation. This disease in TCM pertains to the categories "re ru xueshi" (invasion of the blood chamber by heat), "dai xiai" (leukorrhagia), "zheng jiai" (mass in the abdomen), etc.

Point
Guilai (ST 29)

Location
Guilai (ST 29) acupoint is located 4 *cun* below the umbilicus, 2 *cun* lateral to Zhongji (RN 3) (See Fig. 30).

Method
Acupressure therapy is used. The patient lies in a relaxed supine position, with raised knees. Press and rotate in a circular outward motion immediately around Guilai (ST 29) for 100 times, and then press and rotate in a circular inward motion immediately around Guilai (ST 29) for 100 times. Afterwards, press directly on Guilai (ST 29) for 50 times. Treatment should be self-administered by the patient before sleep every day.

Result
37 cases were treated by this method; the patients averaged four years with chronic pelvic inflammation; after treatment between 9 and 46 times, averaging 25.03 times, 20 cases were completely cured; 12 cases were improved; five of the cases had no change.

Case

Zhang xx, female, 43 years of age, worker. Zhang had low abdominal and low back pain, as well as foul red leukorrhagia for three years. All of these symptoms had become severe in the last week, to the point that they were unbearable by the time she came to the clinic. She found it difficult to walk. Her pain was worse with palpation. TCM diagnosis was chronic pelvic inflammation due to stagnation of *qi* and blood. After using acupressure for 22 times, her pain was gone, and upon a physical check-up, her condition was relieved. The condition did not return for at least one year of follow-up.

Discussion

The point Guilai (ST 29) is on the Yangming (Stomach) Meridian. The Yangming Meridian channels more blood and *qi* than any other meridian in the body. In addition, Guilai (ST 29) is in the local area of the problem, and is therefore even more effective. By applying acupressure on this point, will aid the circulation of *qi* and blood in the area, to remove any stagnation. Where there is stagnation, there is pain; and when the stagnation is gone, so is the pain.

4.6. Morning Sickness

Morning sickness or pernicious vomiting is marked by a group of symptoms including nausea, vomiting, dizziness, anorexia within the first trimester of gestation. It is a commonly seen disorder appearing in early stage of pregnancy. Severe condition may emaciate the pregnant woman very quickly and trigger off other diseases.

Point
Shenmen (EP-I 1)

Location

Shenmen (EP-I 1) auricular point is located at bifurcating point between superior and inferior antihelix crus, and at the lateral 1/3 of triangular fossa (See Fig. 19).

Method

Auricular puncture is used. Press very small, 3mm needles into the point Shenmen (auricular point, EP-I 1) bilaterally. Cover the needles with plaster 5 mm square, to hold inside for three days before changing to a new one. Stop treatment when the problem ceases, usually not more than two weeks, five changes. In addition, the patient is to press the needle with her fingers 50 times on each point in the morning, afternoon and evening. If she feels nauseous or discomfort, she may also press the needles during the discomfort.

Result

124 cases were treated with this method. 64 cases were completely cured with one treatment; 39 cases were completely cured with two treatments; 21 cases were completely cured with three treatments; 96 of the 124 cases were asked about side effects and felt nothing.

Discussion

Shenmen (auricular point EP-I 1) can stimulate the auricular branch of vagus nerves, to control and regulate digestive muscles.

4.7. Abnormal Position of Fetus

Abnormal position of fetus means the fetus is in an abnormal position in the uterus after thirty weeks of pregnancy. It is often seen in multipara or pregnant women who have laxity of the abdominal wall. The pregnant woman herself has no subjective symptoms and precise diagnosis is confirmed by the breech position or transverse position on obstetric examination.

Point

Zhiyin (BL 67)

Location

Zhiyin (BL 67) is located on the lateral side of the small toe, about 0.1 *cun* from the corner of the nail (See Fig. 2).

Method

Moxibustion is used. Gentle moxibustion, with a moxa stick, is used with the patient sitting in a backed chair, in a very relaxed position; her belt should be open and her feet on a stool. Move the moxa stick around the point bilaterally, in the sparrow pecking method for 20 minutes once or twice a day. Seven days is one course.

Result

100 cases were treated with this method. 71 cases were successful; 29 cases had no result. Most of those who had results did in the first three days. Twenty-four cases were successful in the first day, 17 cases were successful the second day, 13 cases were successful after the third day, 9 cases were successful after four or five days, 5 cases were successful after six or seven days of treatment, 3 cases were successful after eight to nine days.

Case

Li xx, female, 23 years of age, seven months pregnant with her first baby, found that the abdominal wall was very tight. The baby and the liquid were normal, but the baby's position was horizontal. Traditional Chinese Medicine diagnosis is abnormal position of fetus due to imbalance of Chong and Ren meridians. Gentle moxibustion was used with this method for 15 minutes in the clinic, after which, the patient continued self-treatment at home once a day for three days. After that, the baby's position changed to normal. The baby was born normal in the 38th week.

Discussion

Abnormal position of fetus has a close relation with kidney *qi*. *Qi* controls blood, which is the foundation for women. When *qi* and blood are balanced, the position of the baby will be normal. The baby grew through the Chong, Ren, and Dai meridians. These three meridians also have a close relationship with the kidney. The kidney and the urinary bladder are internal and external meridians that affect each other. Zhiyin (BL 67) point belongs to the urinary bladder meridian and has the function to regulate kidney *qi*, so stimulating this point can harmonize the Chong, Ren and Dai meridians. When all are balanced, the baby's position will also be normalized.

4.8. Prolonged-Difficult Labor

Prolonged-difficult labor refers to hypodynamic contraction of uterus during the labor. Clinical manifestations are short time of uterus contractions, irregular, interval long, mouth of uterus opening wide no enough, baby difficult delivery, All of which lead to prolonged difficult labor during labor.

Point

Hegu (LI 4)

Location

Hegu (LI 4) acupoint is located on the dorsum of the hand, between the 1st and 2nd metacarpal bones, approximately in the middle of the 2nd metacarpal bone on the radial side (See Fig. 46).

Method

Electric acupuncture is used on Hegu (LI 4). The woman lies in a supine position with both legs up. Insert 1.5 *cun* needles bilaterally perpendicular to the point, 1.2 *cun* deep, directed to the point Huoxi (SI 3). When the patient feels a *qi* sensation, use an electric stimulator in the continuous wave pattern. Continue this treatment until the baby is born.

Result

30 cases were treated in this method; in from 5-10 minutes, the uterine muscles started to relax and open, making the delivery easier for the mother.

Case

Zhao xx, female, 43 years old, was pregnant with her fourth child. She had a difficult labor when the cervix did not open wide enough. After treatment with this method for one-half hour, her contractions became intense and the baby was delivered.

Discussion

The point Hegu (LI 4) belongs to Yangming (large intestine) meridian. Hegu (LI 4) is the Yuan primary point for this meridian. It can treat difficult labor and strengthen the uterine muscle. Only use it with a pregnant when she is in labor.

4.9. Postpartum Retention of Urine

Postpartum retention of urine, the most of which due to difficult labor lead to disorder of nerval function resulting in large amounts of urine accumulated in the bladder. Clinically characterized by blockage of urine and distension and fullness in the lower abdomen.

Point

Shenque (RN 8)

Location

Shenque (RN 8) is located in the center of the umbilicus (See Fig. 26).

Method

Moxibustion is used. Indirect moxibustion with salt is used. The patient lies in a supine position. Take 20 g of salt, stir-fry until it turns yellow, and fill the navel to completely cover the umbilicus. Two to three cm in diameter should be enough. Then ground two ground green onions into a paste and form a cake 0.3 mm high, to sit on top of the salt. Finally, place a large moxa cone on top of the green onion cake. Let burn, usually more than halfway, until the patient has the desire to urinate, or the moxa cone becomes too hot for the patient to tolerate. Replace the moxa cones until the patient has the desire to urinate. Three to five moxa cones should be sufficient. One treatment is a one course.

Result

19 cases were treated by this method. 10 cases were completely cured. All of these 10 cases only needed one moxa cone for their treatment. Five cases were cured after using three or four moxa cones; one case had the desire to urinate four hours after treatment. Another case was treated again on the following day with three moxa cones, before having the desire to urinate. Two cases had three treatments with no result.

Case

Luo xx, female, 25 years of age. After labor, Luo had no desire to urinate for two days. First she was treated by an injection of Western medicine, without any result. The doctor inserted a urinary catheter; it was drained every four hours. After using three moxa cones in one treatment, the patient felt the need to urinate. The second day, two moxa cones were used to finish the treatment, after which time, she was able to urinate by herself.

4.10. Postpartum Complications

After delivery, the mother feels nervous, angry, thinks too much, looses blood, and also feels weak and tired. All of these symptoms lead to insomnia.

Point

Baihui (DU 20)

Location

Baihui (DU 20) acupoint is located on the head, 5 *cun* directly above the midpoint of the anterior hairline, approximately on the midpoint of the line connecting the apexes of both ears (See Fig. 4).

Method

Moxibustion is used with the patient in a sitting position. Divide the hair on top of the head to expose the point. Use moxa stick above the point in a sparrow pecking and circular motion before sleep for 15 minutes. Four constitute one course. Use as long as necessary.

Result

21 cases were treated with this method. Most of the patients could sleep after 15 minutes of treatment; a few patients could sleep after a few hours; some patients fell asleep during the treatment. Patients generally sleep fitfully for 8-12 hours.

Case

Luo xx, female 23 years old, had a difficult labor, lost a lot of blood. She could not sleep for two days or nights. She took Western medicine, barbiturates, to sleep both orally and by injection, without effect. The first time she was treated by this method, she fell asleep for six hours, two hours after treatment. After the second treatment, she fell asleep for eight hours after 30 minutes of treatment. With the third treatment, she fell asleep while being treated, and stayed asleep for nine hours.

Discussion

Baihui (DU 20) acupoint belongs to the Du Meridian. The Du Meridian controls all the Yang meridians of the body. After labor, a woman tends to be *qi* and blood deficient, because of the loss of blood. Baihui (DU 20) can increase Yang and *qi*, to quiet the mother's mind.

4.11. Hypogalactia (Lactation Insufficiency)

Hypogalactia or gaglactia refers to very little or no milk secreted from the puerpera breast. Clinical manifestation is scanty or absence of milk secretion after childbirth, or continuous decrease in quantity during lactation. It is commonly known as "Deficient Lactation".

Point
Danzhong (Shanzhong) (RN 17)

Location

Danzhong (RN 17) acupoint is located on the anterior midline, at the level with the fourth intercostal space, midway between the nipples (See Fig. 26).

Method

Acupuncture and moxibustion are used with the patient lying in a supine position. Use a needle two *cun* in length in a horizontal direction facing down towards the feet 1.5 *cun* deep. When the patient feels a *qi* sensation, leave the needles untouched for 30-60 minutes, depending on the severity of the case. Cold or excess syndromes need to keep the needles in longer time. If the patient is deficient or hot, the needles stay in for a short time. In the case that a woman is both deficient and cold, the needles can stay in longer. For deficient or cold syndromes, follow needling with gentle moxibustion using a moxa stick in the sparrow pecking method for 20 minutes.

Result

20 cases were treated with this method; sufficient milk was produced after the first treatment in 14 cases; sufficient milk was produced after the second treatment in five cases; one case received sufficient milk after the third treatment.

Case

Gui xx, female, 24 years of age, worker. After labor, she felt breast distension and pain, had difficulty excreting milk, was depressed and nervous. Her tongue was red with a yellow coating. Her pulse was wiry. TCM Diagnosis is lactation insufficiency due to stagnation of liver *qi*. After two treatments using this method, milk came smoothly to nourish the baby.

Discussion

Danzhong (RN 17) is one of eight connecting points. It is a special point to connect *qi* from one place to another. *Qi* can regulate milk and stimulate the endocrine gland. If there is *qi* deficiency or stagnant *qi*, it can either cause deficient milk or cause stagnation so that it is difficult to release. Stimulating Danzhong (RN 17) regulates *qi* circulation, so milk can flow smoothly.

4.12. Childhood Mumps

Childhood mumps (epidemic parotitis or mumps) is an

acute infection disease. It is defined as an acute, general and non-suppurative disease caused by the mumps virus. Its characteristics are swelling and pain of the parotid gland.

Point
Jiaosun (SJ 20)

Location
Jiaosun (SJ 20) is located directly above the ear apex, within the hairline (See Fig. 3).

Methods
1. Acupressure is used. Use the thumb and index finger to pinch the point from both directions bilaterally 50 times, as strongly as the baby can bear. The treatment is done once daily. Three treatments constitute one course.

2. Burning therapy is used. Stick a small piece of cotton, soaked in cooking oil, on the bottom end of a match. Clean the local area, cut hair around the point, and light the cotton. After the fire has gone out, touch the cotton to the skin at Jiaosun (SJ 20) point. As soon as you hear a sound, quickly remove the cotton from the point. The burnt area should be 0.5 cm square. After a few days, a scar will develop. Keep the local area dry; it will heal on its own.

3. Bleeding therapy is used. Insert the three-edged needle on the problem side one to three times. 0.2-0.5 ml. of blood should be released. When finished, use dry cotton to close the hole. One treatment is sufficient. If after two days there is no change, repeat the treatment.

Results

Method 1. 12 cases were treated by the first method. After one course, all cases were completely cured.

Method 2. 334 cases were treated by the second method. 312 cases were completely cured; 5 cases improved; 17 cases showed no effect.

Method 3. Usually one time can treat all symptoms; two or three treatments completely cure the patients.

Cases

1. Guo xx, male, 6 years old. Guo had mumps on the left side, distension and swelling below the ear, he cannot open his mouth easily. The skin color around the area is normal, and pain is increased with pressure. TCM diagnosis is childhood mumps due to wind heat. He was treated by the first method three times and completely cured.

2. Wang xx, male, 4 years old. Wang had mumps on both sides, pressing the tendon. He could not eat. His TCM diagnosis was childhood mumps due to wind heat. After 30 minutes of treatment on both sides by the second method, Wang could eat fruit and drink water. The next day, after no further treatment, he was completely cured.

3. Chen xx, male, 5 years old. Chen had mumps on the right side for two days. He was swollen, felt heat and felt pain when touched. In addition, he had fever, headache, and difficulty opening his mouth. TCM diagnosis is childhood mumps due to wind heat. After one treatment by the third method, pain and fever were gone; his mumps were completely cured after three treatments.

Discussion

Method one is appropriate for mild cases; methods two and three are appropriately used for severe cases; method two only needs to be done once.

4.13. Infantile Diarrhea

Infantile diarrhea refers to increased frequency and volume of defecation. Acute diarrhea may be associated with improper intake, bacterial infection by its toxin, or viral infection. The course of diarrhea of persisting type is usually over four weeks and it is often caused by uncontrolled intestinal infections or induced by flora imbalance resulting from abused antibiotics.

Point
Shenque (RN 8)

Location

Shenque (RN 8) is located in the center of the umbilicus (See Fig. 26).

Method

Medicated compress therapy is used. Make an herbal formula of equal amounts of ground herbs including Ganjiang (Dried Ginger, *Rhizoma Zingieris*); Fuzi (Prepared Lateral Roor of Aconite, *Radix Aconiti Lateralis Prasparata*); Wuzhuyu, (Evodia Fruit, *Fructus Euodiae*), mix into a thick paste with vinegar. Fill the navel with the paste and cover the umbilicus with a 4 cm square plaster. Change it after three days. Be careful keep the area dry; do not to wash near the plaster.

Result

32 cases were treated in this way. 31 cases were completely cured; one case did not change. Of the 31 cases, 21 cases were cured after two days of treatment; 8 cases were cured after three days of treatment; 2 cases were cured after five days of treatment.

Case

Ai xx, female, 6 months old. Ai had diarrhea seven to nine times every day for 15 days. Undigested food was found in the stools. She was thin, had a sallow complexion, and poor appetite. Her tongue was light red with a slightly thick, sticky white coating. Traditional Chinese Medicine diagnosis was diarrhea due to deficient *qi* and spleen Yang. On the second day of this treatment, Ai's diarrhea reduced to three or four times in the day. The third day, she produced a normal stool twice.

Discussion

Shenque (RN 8) acupoint belongs to the Ren Meridian. It has a special function to strengthen the spleen and stomach. Two of the herbs used here, Fuzi and Wuzhuyu improve Yang; Ganjiang removes cold from the meridians. Improving Yang and removing cold has the result of stopping the diarrhea.

4.14. Enuresis

Enuresis of children is defined as involuntary emptying of the bladder during the daytime or at night when the children are above the age of three. Main manifestations: involuntary urination during sleep with dreams several times a night or once in several nights. In protracted cases, there are accompanying symptoms of sallow complexion, anorexia and lassitude. This disease is categorized as "yi niao" (bed-wetting) in TCM.

Point
Yiniao (Experience Point)

Location
Yiniao (experience point) is located in the middle of the most distal crease of the small toe (See Fig. 47).

Method
Acupuncture is used on Yiniao point bilaterally. Sterilize with 75% alcohol. Insert while rotating 0.5 *cun* needles, until the tip of the needle touches the bone. Manually manipulate (rotate) the needle strongly, until the patient feels severe pain in the local area, heat and distension to the lower abdomen. Leave the needles untouched for 30 minutes. Treatment should be done once daily. Five treatments constitute one course.

Result
10 cases were treated by this method. 5 cases were completely cured after one treatment; 3 cases were completely cured after two treatments; 2 cases were completely cured after three treatments.

Case
Zhao xx, female, 15 years old, a student. Zhao had enuresis every day or every other day for 10 years. She was treated by many methods without any result. When she was given acupuncture, she improved after one treatment. The same night that

she was treated, she ate watermelon, and did not urinate. And then, she was treated two courses and completely cure. Enuresis has not returned in seven years of follow-up.

Discussion

The most important thing here is patient cooperation. During the treatment, children are advised to limit their activity and avoid drinking liquids or eating watery fruits before bed. In addition, regular (fixed) bed times, and toilet schedules are important, especially at night.

4.15. Excessive Night Crying

Excessive night crying in children means the baby is normal in the daytime, but interval or continuous crying during all the night. It may be caused by abdominal pain, abdominal distension, itching in anus, over eating; in attach, indigestive, disorder of nerve system. All of which lead to the baby excessive crying.

Point
Zhongchong (PC 9)

Location

Zongchong (PC 9) acupoint is located in the center of the tip of the middle finger (See Fig. 48).

Method

Bleeding therapy is used. The three-edge needle method is used. Sterilize the area of Zhongchong (PC 9) point on one side first; apply treatment. Insert the three-edge needle 0.1 *cun*. Four drops of blood should be released. Usually one treatment can get a good result. If treatment is not successful on that side, the next day use the three-edge needle method on Zhongchong (PC 9) on the other side. Two treatments should be enough to solve the problem.

Result

49 cases were treated by this method. 46 cases were completely cured; three cases found no change.

Case

Zhou xx, female, 3 years old. During the daytime, she acted normally. At night, Zhou cried all night without reason. After she was treated once by the three-edged needle method, she was completely cured of night crying.

Chapter V
Ophthalmic, Ear-Nose-Throat
Diseases and others

5.1. Hordeolum

Hordeolum, or a common style, is a kind of suppurative in-flammation of the eyelid gland. After suppuration, its pus head is whitish-yellow in color, in the shape of a ripe wheat-seed, so in TCM it is called "mai li zhong" (hordeolum). If tarsadenitis occurs, after suppuration, a pus can be seen on the surface of palpebral conjuunctiva, which is known as 'nei mai li zhong" (internal hordeollum). TCM gives the former the name "tou zhen" or "zhen yan" and the latter "nei zhen yan".

Point
Ear Apex (EP-K 12)

Location

Ear apex (EP-K 12) auricular point is located at the upper tip auricle and superior to helix when folded towards tragus (See Fig. 19).

Method

Do bleeding therapy on the affected side with three-edge needles. Quickly insert into auricular apex (EP-K 12) 0.1 *cun* and produce between 10-15 drops of blood. When finished, close hole with dry cotton. Usually one treatment is enough. If not, treatment may be repeated for two or three times.

Result

102 cases were treated by this method. 91 cases were cured with one treatment; 5 cases were cured after two treatments; 6 cases were unchanged.

Case

Chen xx, female, 10 years old, student. The outer edge of the left upper eye had a small knot in it the size of a grain of rice. Her eye was red, swollen, distended, and painful around the affected area. TCM diagnosis was hordeolum due to heat in the Stomach Meridian. She was cured after one treatment by this method. The day after treatment, all the symptoms were gone.

Discussion

This disease usually results from heat in the Yangming Meridian. All Yang meridians connect on the ear, so this point can clear heat from all Yang meridians.

5.2. Lacrimation (Tearing)

Lacrimation means tearing, which is caused by dacryagogatresia or hyperactitve function of lacrimal secretion. Lacrimation in traditional Chinese medicine refers to a constant running of tears, especially when exposed to wind, even though there is neither redness nor pain in the eyes. It is a common eye disorder, mostly bother the elderly, similar to dystopy of lacumal punctum, daciycystitis, canaliculitis, trachoma and chronic conjunctivitis in Western medicine.

Point
Taiyang (EX-HN 5)

Location

Taiyang (EX-HN 5) extra point is located in the depression about one fingerbreadth posterior to the midpoint between the lateral end of the eyebrow and the outer canthus (See Fig. 49).

Method

Acupuncture and cupping are used on the problem side. Use 1.0 *cun* needles. Perpendicularly insert by rotating the needle into Taiyang (EX-HN 5) 0.8 *cun* deep. When the patient feels a *qi* sensation around the eye, leave the needle for 20-30 minutes. After needling, do cupping for about 15 minutes, using small cups.

Result

27 cases or 51 eyes were treated with this method; some patients had a problem in one eye, and others had a problem in both eyes simultaneously. 22 of these cases, with 41 problem eyes, or 80.4%, were completely cured after one treatment. Three cases, with 6 problem eyes, 11.7%, were improved after one treatment. The remaining 2 cases, with 4 problem eyes, 7.9%, did not change.

Case

Yang xx, male, 38 years old. Both of Yang's eyes were treated continuously for two years, worsening in the winter. He was hesitant to go outside or ride a bicycle. Treatment by herbs and Western medicine had no effect. After being treated once by this combined acupuncture and cupping method, he was completely cured.

5.3. Optic Atrophy

Optic atrophy is a chronic eye disorder marked by gradual degeneration of the vision acuity. At the early stage there is only blurring of vision, but at the late stage the eyesight may be totally lost.

Point
Xinming (Experience Point)

Location

Xinming (experience point) is located in the center of the crease behind the ear, 0.5 *cun* superior and anterior to Yifeng (SJ 17) (See Fig. 50).

Method

Acupuncture therapy is used. Flatten the ear forward and take 1.5 *cun* needles at an oblique angle, 45°C into the crease, and insert 1 *cun*.   Manipulate with the reinforcing method. Lift and thrust, while rotating, until a *qi* sensation reaches the eye. Leave the needles untouched for 30 minutes.

Result

698 cases with 1,252 problem eyes were treated by this method. 103 eyes were completely cured; 112 eyes were very much improved; 586 eyes were improved; 451 eyes were unchanged. The total effective rate was 63.98%.

Case

Yang xx, female, 10 years old, a student. Her right eye had a nervous problem, leading to unclear vision, for six years. Western medicine diagnosed her as having right eye optic atrophy. TCM diagnosis was deficiency of *qi* and blood. Using this method 100 times, her vision clarity increased 0.4 and she was able to a wide scope, where she had previously tunnel vision.

5.4. Myopia

Myopia is an ametropic condition in ophthalmology. It is mainly characterized by the fact that eyes can see near objects but not distant ones, although there is no abnormality with the outer eyes. Such a condition often bothers youngsters.

Point

Eye (EP-A 10)

Location

Eye (EP-A 10) auricular point is located in the 5th section of ear lobe. (See Fig. 19).

Method

Auricular acupuncture therapy is used. Small press needles, 3 mm, are placed bilaterally into the point and covered with 5 mm square of plaster. Every day, the patient needs to press the needles 50 times on each point three times daily, morning, afternoon and evening. With each pressing, the patient should close the eyes. After pressing the ear point, focus on a far subject for 10 minutes. After five days, change the needles and plaster. Ten treatments constitute one course. Rest one week between courses. Only two courses should be necessary.

Result

500 cases were treated with this method. 48 cases were completely cured; 146 cases were much improved; 218 cases were improved; 88 cases showed no change. The total effectiveness of this treatment was 82%. Completely cured indicates vision above 1.0; much improved indicates vision above 0.8; improved indicates vision above 0.6.

Case

Li xx, male, 11 years old, student. Li's vision has been decreasing for one year. Vision in his right eye tested at 0.1; vision in his left eye tested at 0.5. After one course of this treatment method, both of Li's eyes tested at 1.5. He did a second course of treatments. Li's eyes were tested again six months later at 1.5.

Discussion

This method is suitable for patients less than 18 years old; however, is more successful with patients less than 12 years old.

5.5. Deafness

Deafness, a sensorineural hearing loss, occurs abruptly for reasons unknown. Its main clinical feature is a sudden profound sensorineural deafness, accompanied by tinnitus and dizziness, and a tendency to get cured spontaneously. The disorder is usually unilateral and occurs more often in females and mostly in the middle-aged.

Point
Tinggong (SI 19)

Location

Tinggong (SI 19) acupoint is located anterior to the tragus and posterior to the condyliod process of the mandible, in the depression formed when the mouth is open (See Fig. 3).

Method

Acupuncture is used. Acupuncture is done with the patient in the sitting position. Firstly, the patient opens his/her mouth as wide as possible. The acupuncturist inserts 1.5 *cun* needles perpendicularly about 1.0 *cun*, towards the other ear. After the acupuncturist finishes inserting the needles, the patient can close his/her mouth. Leave the needles in the ear for 30 minutes. Secondly, during this time, the patient is to press his/her nose with the thumb and forefinger, breath in through the mouth, and force air out of their ears. It works best when some sound can be heard escaping from the ear. 10 treatments are one course.

Result

Acute cases can get good results in one or two treatments. Chronic cases usually need more than 10 treatments to obtain a good result.

Case

Lu xx, male, 40 years old, a farmer. Lu's health was basically good, but he was nervous and drank a lot of alcohol. Lu was known to be argumentative with somebody. After arguments, he felt headache, dizziness and suddenly loses his hearing. TCM diagnosis was nervous deafness due to hyperactivity of liver Yang. After five treatments by this method, Lu was completely cured.

Discussion

This method is suitable for nervous deafness, without any organic problems.

5.6. Tinnitus

Tinnitus is characterized by ringing sound in the ears felt by the patient. Main manifestations: distension sensation and ringing in the ears that can not be eliminated by pressing, irritability and hot temper; or intermittent tinnitus aggravated by strain and eliminated by pressing, dizziness, soreness and aching of the lower back, seminal emission, excessive leukorrhea.

Point

Yemen (SJ 2)

Location

Yemen (SJ 2) acupoint is located when the fist is clenched; the point is located in the depression proximal to the margin of the web between the ring and small fingers, at the junction of the red and white skin (See Fig. 25).

Method

Acupuncture with 1*cun* needles is used. Insert horizontally to the metacarpal bone, about 1 *cun* deep. Rotate about 10 times or until the patient feels a *qi* sensation up the arm. Leave the needles for 30-60 minutes. Every 10 minutes manipulate the needles. During this time, the patient is to press his/her nose with the thumb and forefinger, breath in through the mouth, and force air out of their ears. It works best when some sound can be heard escaping from the ear. 10 treatments are one course.

Result

204 cases were treated by this method. 80 cases were completely cured, 52 cases were much improved, 52 cases improved, 20 cases showed no change. Total effectiveness of this method was 91%.

Case

Wu xx, female, 25 years old. Wu had heard ringing in her ears for more than one month, without any reason. She went to a Western Ear, Nose and Throat doctor, with no discovery of cause. TCM diagnosis was tinnitus due to Sanjiao fire. While the acupuncturist was manipulating the needle using this treatment method, the patient felt a hot sensation in the ear. After treatment, the ringing in her ears decreased and she was able to hear better. Four more treatments were done before she was completely cured of her tinnitus.

5.7. Meniere's Disease

Meniere's disease is also known as hydrops of membranous labyrinth. Its clinical characteristics are paroxysmal dizziness, fluctuating deafness, tinnitus and a feeling of fullness in the ear. It belongs to the category of "xuan yun" (dizziness) in TCM.

Point

Baihui (DU 20)

Location

Baihui (DU 20) acupoint is located on the midline of the

head, 5 *cun* directly above the midpoint of the anterior hairline, approximately on the midpoint of the line connecting the apexes of both ears (See Fig. 4).

Method

Moxibustion is used. Direct moxibustion non-scarring method is used. The patient sits in a chair. Cut the hair 1 cm around the point. Smooth vaseline on the point. Use about 50 small moxa cones, the size of a grain of rice. The treatment will take about one hour. One treatment should be enough. A scab will form and fall away within a month.

Result

177 cases were treated with this method. 156 cases were completely cured; 19 cases were improved; 2 cases showed no change. Total effectiveness of this treatment was 98.88%.

Case

Zhou xx, male, 60 years old, worker. Suddenly he felt dizziness, tinnitus, vomiting. TCM diagnosis was Meniere's disease due to deficiency of *qi* and blood. After one treatment, using 50 moxa cones by this method, he felt better. No symptoms returned for the five years of follow-up.

Discussion

Meniere's disease is usually due to deficiency of *qi* and blood, or deficiency of kidney essence. The point Baihui (DU 20) has a special function to strengthen Yin and Yang, to balance *qi*, blood, and kidney essence.

5.8. Rhinitis

Rhinitis is including acute rhinitis, chronic rhinitis, atrophic rhinitis, and allergic rhinitis. Acute rhinitis is an acute infective inflammation of the nasal mucosa. Its clinical features are a feeling of burning heat in the nose, nasal obstruction, sneezing, rhinorrhea, headache, fever, etc. Chronic rhinitis is a chronic inflammatory change of the nasal mucosa, mainly due to the protraction of acute rhinitis. Its main symptom is nasal obstruction. Atrophic rhinitis is a chronic atrophic change of the nasal mucosa, periost and nasal cavity with crusts on it, coryza foetida and hyposmia. Allergic rhinitis is an allergic disease caused by the sensitinogen acting on the mucous membranes of the nasal cavity, also called perennial allergic rhinitis, Clinically it has the following features: itching in the nose, sneeze, watery nasal discharge, nasal obstruction coming and going suddenly.

Point
Yingxiang (LI 20)

Location
Yingxiang (LI 20) acupoint is located in the nasolabial groove, at the level of the midpoint of the lateral border of ala nasi (See Fig. 5).

Method
Electric acupuncture is used. Acupuncture with 1.0 *cun* needles is used bilaterally. Insert the needles horizontally 0.8 *cun* deep in the direction of the top of the nose. Rotate both needles at the same time, until the whole nose feels the *qi* sensation. Put electrical device on the tip of the needles, using the strongest continuous wave the patient can bear, for 30 minutes

once daily. Ten treatments are one course.

Result

360 cases with many variations of rhinitis were treated by this method. 176 cases, 49%, were much improved; 142 cases, 39%, were improved; 42 cases, 12%, found no change. This method usually has a better result after 3-5 treatments. The most treatments any of these patients received were 20; the least treatments they received were 8; the average treatment they received was 13.

Case

Cai xx, female, 36 years old, a worker. She felt itching and something inside her nose, and had a runny nose, for three years. Her symptoms worsened in winter. She took a lot of medicines, both Western and Chinese, without result. After one treatment of electric acupuncture, her nose running decreased noticeably. The other symptoms ceased with the completion of a course of treatments.

Discussion

This method is suitable for any kind of rhinitis. Particularly, It is better for chronic rhinitis.

5.9. Epistaxis

Epistaxis means nose bleeds, which is common clinical symptoms, and can be caused by mycteric or general diseases. It is mostly seen in Kiesselbach's area. The naso-nasopharyngeal plexus at the end of the inferior nasal meatus is also an area where nosebleed is apt to occur.   TCM call this symptom "bi nu" (nose bleed), "bi hong" (flood-like nose bleed), "hong hand" (red sweat), etc., all meaning epistaxis.

Point
Shangxing (DU 23)

Location
Shangxing (DU 23) acupoint is located 1 *cun* directly above the midpoint of the anterior hairline (See Fig. 5).

Method
Acupuncture is used. Acupuncture with 2 *cun* needles is used. Insert 1.5 *cun* horizontally towards Baihui (DU 20). Manipulate the needle, by rotating for three minutes every 10 minutes. Leave the needle for 30 minutes.

Result
Bleeding can be stopped during treatment. 17 cases were treated with this method. 16 cases, 95.3%, were stopped during the first session, after an average of about 1.5 minutes; the last case had no change and did not repeat treatment.

Case
Liu xx, male, 35 years old, teacher. He had sudden nose bleeding that wouldn't stop. He tried many methods: cotton, took medicine and had no result. After three minutes of acupuncture treatment at this point, nose bleeding stopped. The needles were left in for only 10 minutes. There was no further bleeding for 30 minutes of observation.

5.10. Acute Tonsillitis

Acute tonsillitis is an acute nonspecific inflammation of the palatal tonsilliae. Its clinical features are fever, headache, sore throat which is aggravated when swallowing, and reddened and swollen palatal tonsilliae.

Point
Shaoshang (LU 11)

Location
Shaoshang (LU 11) acupoint is located on the radial side of the thumb, about 0.1 *cun* posterior to the corner of the nail (See Fig. 51).

Method
Three-edge needle therapy is used. Choose Shaoshang (LU11) on the affected side as the pain; if both sides are painful, bilaterally insert three-edged needles 0.1 *cun*, after sterilizing the point. Press the thumb, wipe blood with an alcohol soaked cotton ball, and repeat until the patient has bled three times. After the last time, press with a dry cotton ball to close the hole. Do therapy once daily; three to five treatments is usually enough.

Result
164 cases were treated with this method. 108, 65.8%, of these cases were completely cured in three to five treatments; 38, 23.2%, of cases improved in six or seven treatments; there was no effect in 18, 11%, of these cases after eight treatments.

Case
Liu xx, male, 12 year old, student. Liu developed tonsillitis

after a common cold, where he felt fever, chills, pain in his throat, and had difficulty eating and drinking. His temperature was 38°C. The local area was swollen and red. His tonsils and mandibular lymph nodes on both sides of the throat were enlarged. Liu's tongue was red with yellow coating; his pulse was superficial and rapid. After his first treatment, Liu's pain and fever decreased; in four bilateral treatments by this method, his tonsillitis was completely cured.

Discussion
1. Shaoshang (LU 11) belongs to the Lung Meridian. The branch of Lung Meridian passes through the throat. Shaoshang (LU 11) is therefore able to clean heat of the Lung Meridian.

2. It is commonly thought that the more blood that is released, the better the effect of the treatment.

5.11. Plum Throat
Plum throat refers to the subjective feeling of a foreign body sensation in the throat, as if the throat were stuck by a piece of plum pit, thus acquiring the term plum throat. The main characteristic is that the patient suffers from constant dry cough and repeated empty swallowing. It is where women feel something stuck in their throat, can not expectorate, feel itching, and nothing is physically found in their throat, which may accompany by fullness sensation in the chest and hypochondriac region, and depression. Adult females often complain it. Referring to Western medicine, it is included in the extent of neurosis, globus hystericus, or plumb pit syndrome.

Point
Tiantu (RN 22)

Location

Tiantu (RN 22) acupoint is located in the center of the suprasternal fossa. (See Fig. 27).

Method

Acupuncture is used with 2 *cun* needles, and the patient is in a sitting position with the head back. First place the needle perpendicularly 0.2 *cun* deep, then change the direction to horizontal, facing downwards, 1.5 *cun* deep, until the patient feels a *qi* sensation inside the throat and chest. At that point, take out the needles.

Result

28 cases were treated with this method. 23 cases were cured after one treatment; 2 cases were cured after three treatments; 3 cases found no change after three treatments.

Case

Liang xx, female, 48 years old, felt something in her throat that she could not get out for three years. When she went to the Western doctor for a physical check-up, she could be found nothing abnormal. TCM diagnosis was *qi* stagnation. Treatment by acupuncture at Tianfu (RN 22) completely cured her problem.

Discussion

This point is the gate of the breath. It can regulate the breath and balance *qi* of the organs. Because this problem is caused by *qi*, Tiantu (RN 22) can eliminate the problem.

5.12. Ulcerative Stomatitis

Ulcerative stomatitis is a kind of scattered superficial small ulcer in the mucous membrane of the mouth, either single or multiple, belonging to the category of "kou gan," or "kou chuang," in TCM, both referring to "ulcer in the mouth" or simply aphtha.

Point

Shenque (RN 8)

Location

Shenque (RN 8) acupoint is located on the middle abdomen and at the center of the umbilicus (See Fig. 26).

Method

Moxibustion is used. Moxibustion with a stick is used about 2 cm above the umbilicus. Move it in a circular motion around the umbilicus, and in the sparrow pecking method for 10 minutes, or until the local area is red, once daily.

Result

104 cases were treated with this method. 58 cases were completely cured after one or two treatments; 30 cases were completely cured after three treatments; 12 cases did not change after three times; 4 cases left without knowledge of any result.

Case

Zhou xx, female, 61 years old, farmer, had ulcerative sores around her lips, severe pain, with the inability to eat and drink. After one treatment of moxibustion, her pain decreased. After two treatments, the pain and the ulcerative areas decreased even further. Complete cure was achieved after five treatments.

5.13. Disturbances Syndrome of Temporomandibular Joint

Disturbances syndrome of temporomandibular joint refers to the area around temporomandibular joint which is painful, distension, soreness, snap, limited of opening mouth, masticatory atonia,etc. Accompanied by dizziness, tinnitus, etc.

Point
Xiaguan (ST 7)

Location
Xiaguan (ST 7) acupoint is located on the face, anterior to the ear, in the depression between the zygomatic arch and mandibular notch (See Fig. 52).

Method
Acupuncture is used with 1 *cun* needles inserted 0.8 *cun* deep. Rotate the needles, lifting and thrusting, until the patient feels a *qi* sensation in the whole local area. Leave the needles for 15 minutes. Do the treatment once daily. One course is 15 treatments.

Result
33 cases were treated by this method. 25 cases were completely cured; 13 cases were improved; 5 cases had no change.

Case
    Qian xx, male, 25 years old, felt joint pain on the right side
of his jaw. When he opened his mouth, you could hear sound
come from the joint, for two weeks. He had limited movement
of his mouth and difficulty eating. Pain was worse with palpation. Treatment by this method completely cured him after eight
sessions.

5.14. Cessation Smoking
    This is an approach through acupuncture treatment to cause
smokers to dislike the smell from cigarette smoking in order to
achieve the purpose of stopping smoking.

Point
Tim Mee (Experience Point)

Location
    Tim Mee (experience point) is located midway between the
two points Yangxi (LI 5) and Lieque (LU 7), in the depression
(See Fig. 53).

Method
    Interdermal (embedding) needles therapy is used. Small
press needles bilaterally and covers with plaster. When the patient feels like smoking, advise them to press the needle 20 times
at each point. During this time, a sweet sensation might be tasted
under the tongue. Leave the needles and plaster on for three days.
They may be changed at that time.

Result

535 cases were treated by this method. 75% of the cases succeeded in quitting smoking after one treatment; an additional 9% of the patients succeeded after two treatments; 16% of the patients did not succeed in quitting smoking.

Case

Lai xx, male 18 year old, worker. He smoked 30 cigarettes daily for three years. He felt dizziness, nausea, tastelessness in the mouth, and had a pale face. Lai decreased his cigarette smoking to 10 a day after one treatment; after two treatments by this method, he totally stopped smoking.

Discussion

The result is better that the patient has to want to stop smoking, and try to control smoking. If the patient does not want to stop smoking, the effects will be nothing.

5.15. Dispelling the Effects of Alcohol

Dispel the effects of alcohol refers to drinking over alcohol; alcoholist feels nausea, vomiting, lethargy or coma, use acupuncture make him awake.

Point

Suliao (DU 25)

Location

Suliao (DU 25) is located on the tip of the nose (See Fig. 31).

Method

Acupuncture is used. Using 0.5 *cun* needles, inserted perpendicularly 0.2 *cun* deep. Stimulate the needles with the reducing method. Leave the needles in for 30 minutes. Every five minutes manipulate the needles.

Result

This method can wake up an unconscious drunk.

Case

An alcoholic patient lost consciousness. He could not speak or control movement. He woke up after using this method of treatment for 10 minutes.

5.16. Reducing Weight

Reducing weight is for obesity. Obesity refers to excessive accumulation of fat in the subcutaneous or other body tissues by at least 15-20% over the normal weight. Clinically, obesity can be divided into simple and secondary types. The former is mainly due to over eating of greasy or sweet food that exceeds the normal consumption of body heat, resulting in the accumulation of fat in the body. Such patients do not present endocrinal dysfunctions pituitary their obesity. Secondary obesity is caused by hypothalamic pituitary lesions and over secretion of hydrocortisone. In the meantime, such patients belong to some neurological and endocrinal dysfunctions.

Point

Guanyuan (RN 4)

Location

Guanyuan (RN 4) acupoint is located on the anterior mid-line, 3 *cun* below the umbilicus (See Fig. 31).

Method

Acupressure is used. Self-application of acupressure is done with the patient lying in a supine position. Press and rotate in a circular motion for 30 minutes once daily, for more than 25 days.

Result

44 cases were treated by this method. 35 cases lost from 1-5 kg after 25 days of treatment; 9 cases did not lose weight.

Case

Zhang xx, male, 42 years old, a worker. The patient had been obese for four years. He weighed 70 kg at 160 cm height. After treating himself by this method, he lost 5kg.

Discussion

The patient's cooperation is required. It is recommended that the patient primarily eats vegetables and little meat, chicken, and sugar. In addition, the patient should do half or an hour of exercises every day.

Appendix
Figures of Acupoints

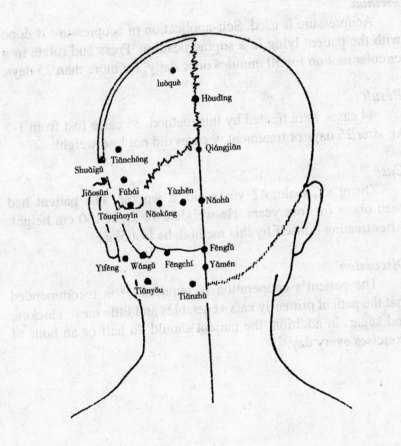

Fig. 1

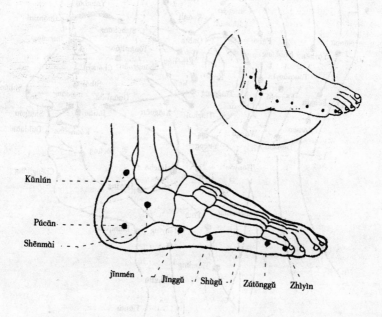

Fig. 2

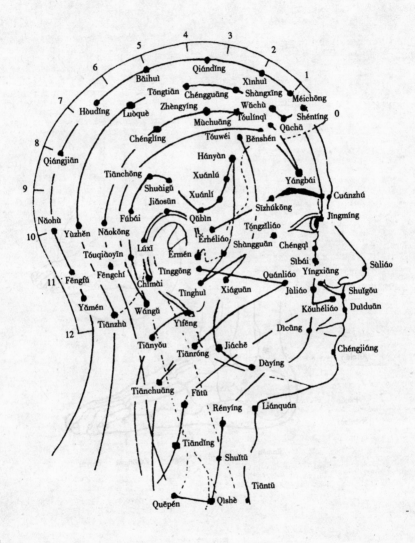

Fig. 3

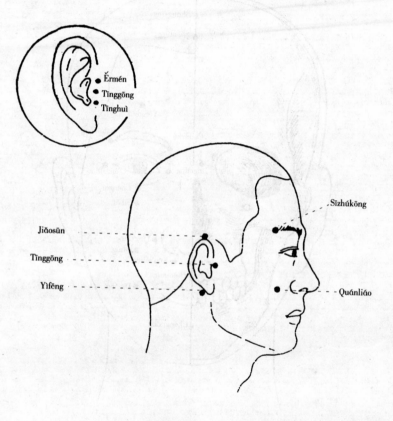

Fig. 4

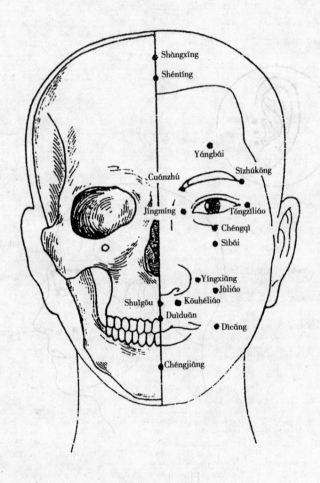

Fig. 5

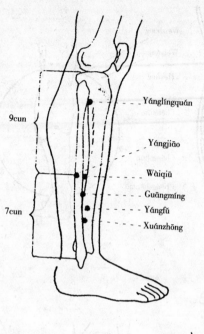

Fig. 6

Yánglíngquán

Yángjiāo

Wàiqiū

Guāngmíng

Yángfǔ

Xuánzhōng

9cun

7cun

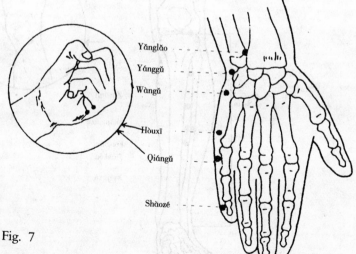

Fig. 7

Yǎnglǎo

Yánggǔ

Wàngǔ

Hòuxī

Qiángǔ

Shàozé

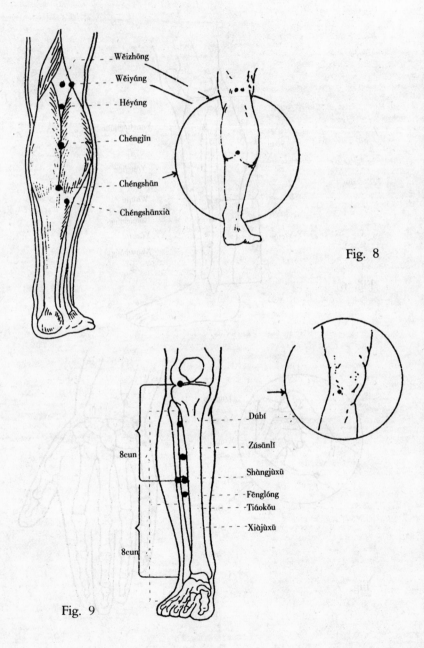

Wěizhōng

Wěiyáng

Héyáng

Chéngjīn

Chéngshān

Chéngshānxià

Fig. 8

8cun

8cun

Dúbí

Zúsānlǐ

Shàngjùxū

Fēnglóng

Tiáokǒu

Xiàjùxū

Fig. 9

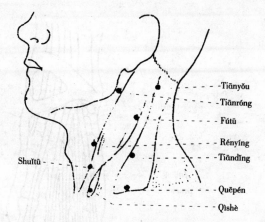

Shuǐtū

Tiānyǒu
Tiānróng
Fútū
Rényíng
Tiāndǐng
Quēpén
Qìshè

Fig. 10

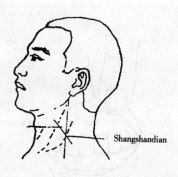

Shangshandian

Fig. 11

173

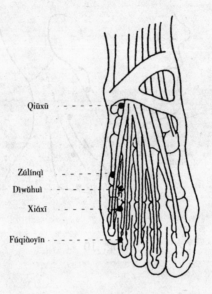

Qiūxū

Zúlínqì
Dìwǔhuì
Xiáxī

Fúqiàoyīn

Fig. 12

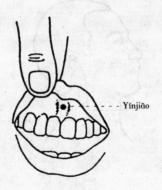

Yínjiāo

Fig. 13

174

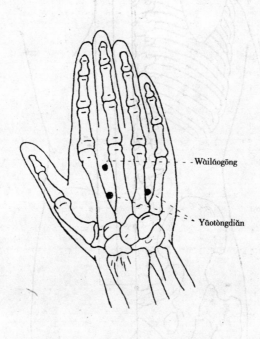

Fig. 14

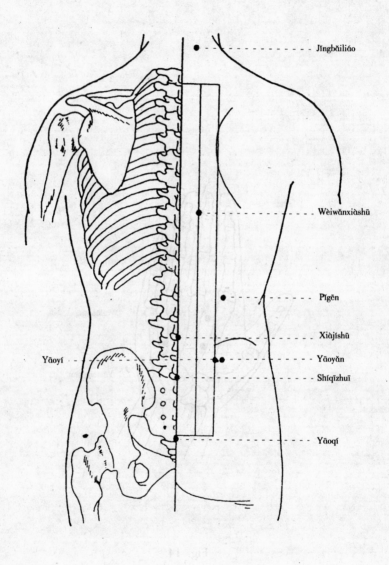

Fig. 15

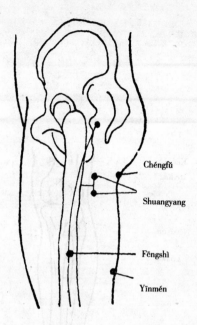

Fig. 16

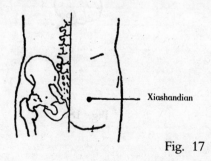

Fig. 17

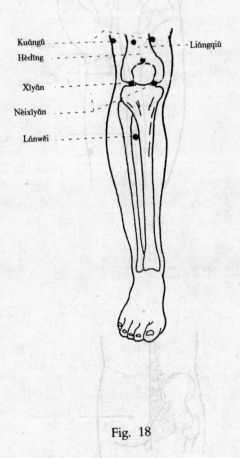

Kuāngǔ

Hèdǐng

Xīyǎn

Nèixīyǎn

Lánwěi

Liángqiū

Fig. 18

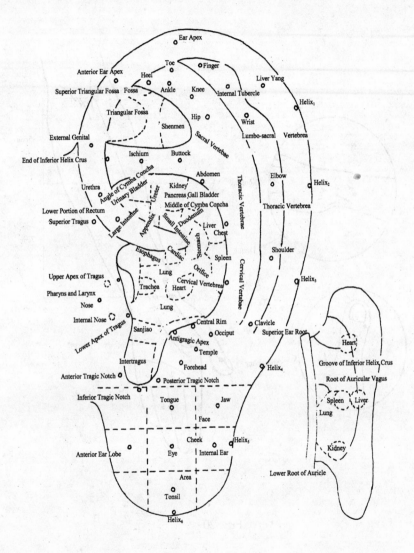

Fig. 19

179

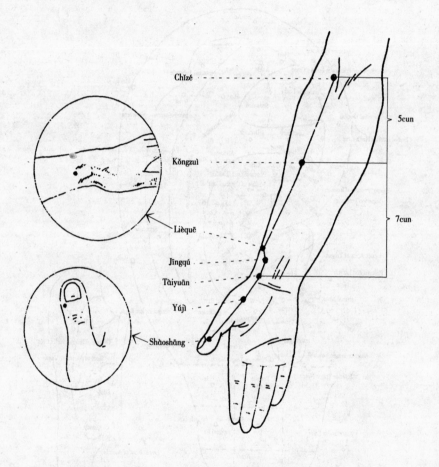

Fig. 20

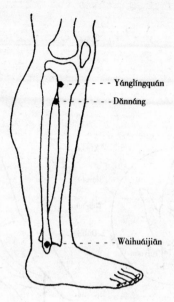

Fig. 21

Yánglíngquán

Dǎnnáng

Wàihuáijiān

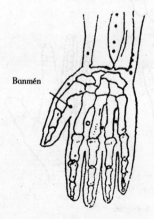

Bǎnmén

Fig. 22

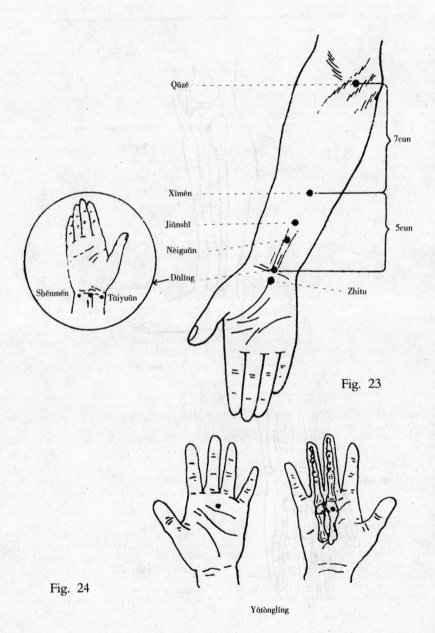

Qūzé

7cun

Xīmén

Jiānshǐ

Nèiguān

5cun

Dàlíng

Zhitu

Shénmén Tàiyuān

Fig. 23

Fig. 24

Yátònglíng

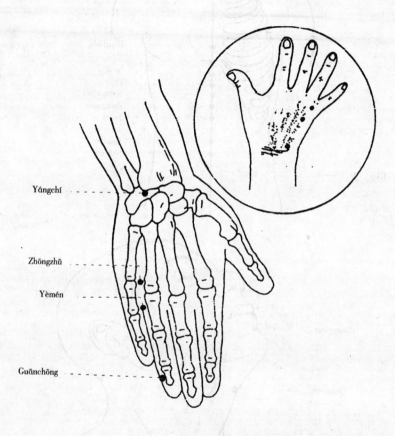

Fig. 25

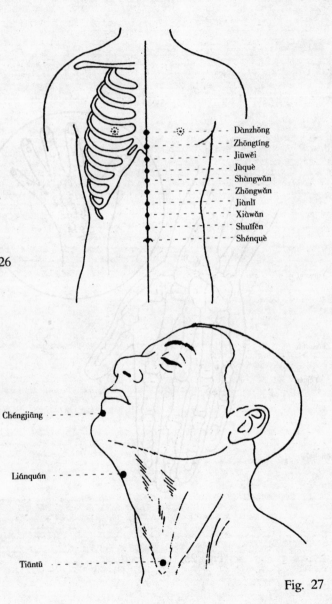

Fig. 26

Dànzhōng
Zhōngtíng
Jiūwěi
Jùquè
Shàngwǎn
Zhōngwǎn
Jiànlǐ
Xiàwǎn
Shuǐfēn
Shénquè

Chéngjiāng
Liánquán
Tiāntū

Fig. 27

184

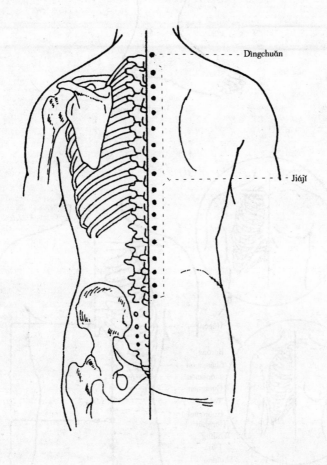

Dìngchuǎn

Jiájǐ

Fig. 28

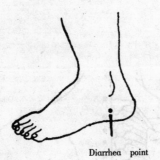

Fig. 29

Diarrhea point

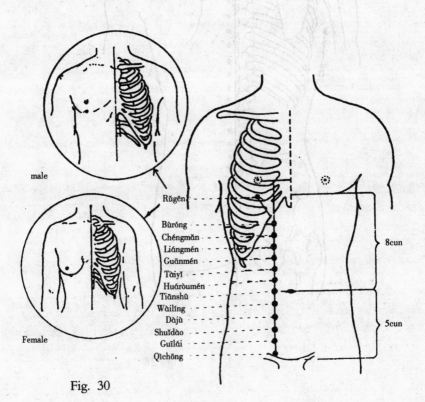

male

Female

Rǔgēn

Bùróng
Chéngmǎn
Liángmén
Guānmén
Tàiyǐ
Huáròumén
Tiānshū
Wàilíng
Dàjù
Shuǐdào
Guīlái
Qìchōng

8cun

5cun

Fig. 30

186

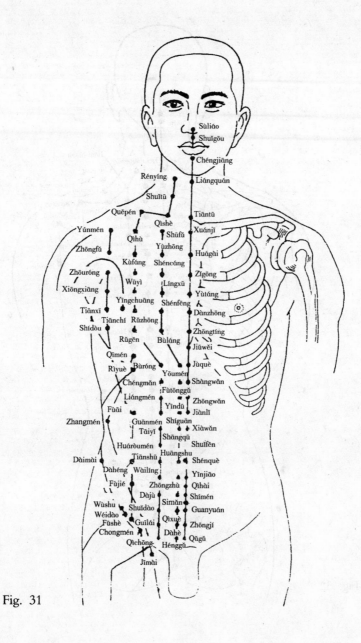

Fig. 31

187

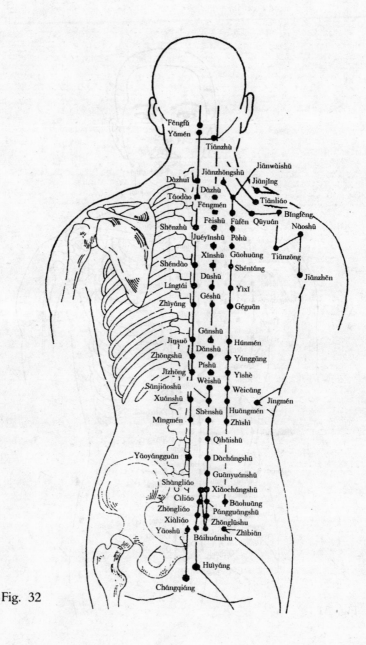

Fig. 32

188

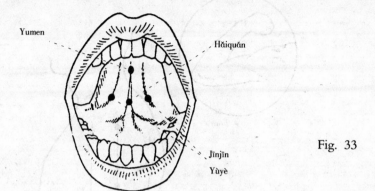

Yumen

Hǎiquán

Jīnjīn
Yùyè

Fig. 33

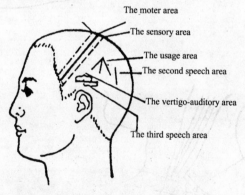

The chorea-trembling controlled area

The moter area

The sensory area

The usage area

The second speech area

The vertigo-auditory area

The third speech area

Fig. 34

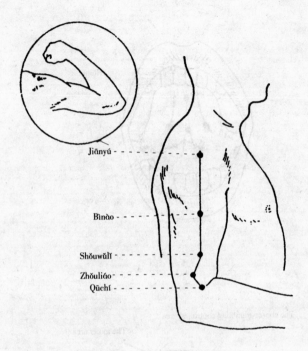

Jiānyú

Bìnào

Shǒuwǔlǐ

Zhǒuliáo

Qūchí

Fig. 35

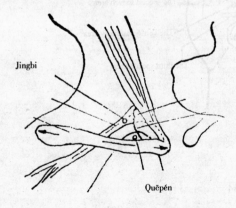

Jingbi

Quēpén

Fig. 36

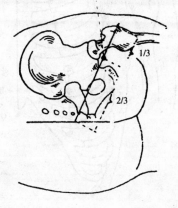

Huántiào

1/3

2/3

Fig. 37

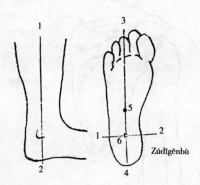

1

3

1 ● 5 2

6

4

2

Zúdǐgēnbù

Fig. 38

191

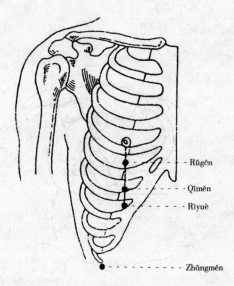

Fig. 39

- Rǔgēn
- Qīmén
- Rìyuè
- Zhāngmén

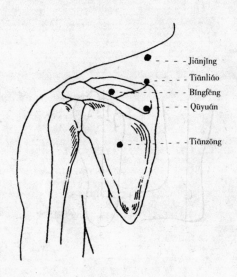

- Jiānjǐng
- Tiānliáo
- Bǐngfēng
- Qūyuán
- Tiānzōng

Fig. 40

192

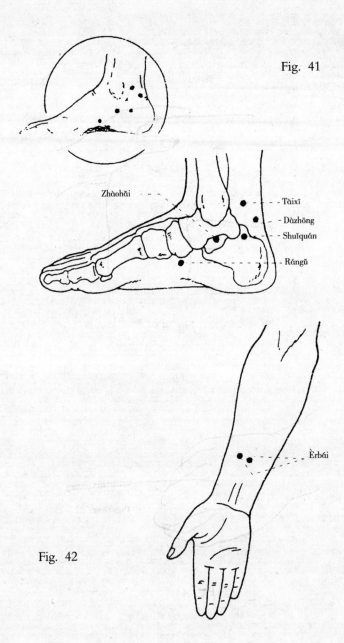

Fig. 41

Zhàohǎi

Tàixī

Dàzhōng

Shuǐquán

Rángǔ

Èrbái

Fig. 42

193

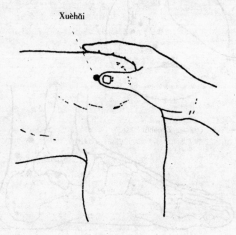

Fig. 43

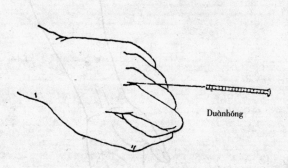

Fig. 44

194

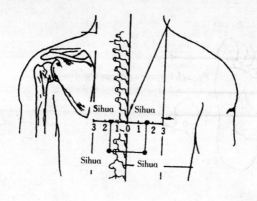

Fig. 45

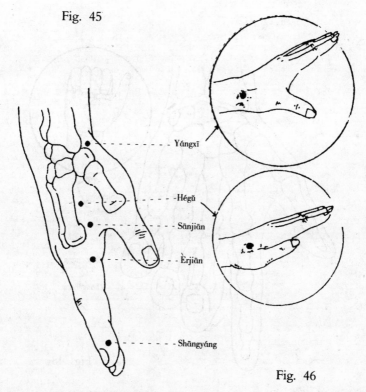

Yángxī

Hégǔ

Sānjiān

Èrjiān

Shāngyáng

Fig. 46

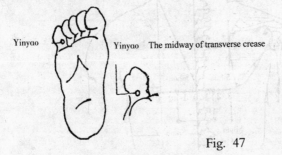

Yinyao   Yinyao   The midway of transverse crease

Fig. 47

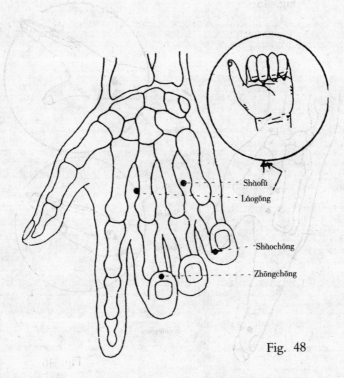

Shàofǔ

Láogōng

Shàochōng

Zhōngchōng

Fig. 48

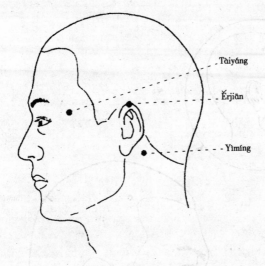

Tàiyáng

Ěrjiān

Yìmíng

Fig. 49

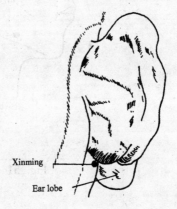

Xinming

Ear lobe

Fig. 50

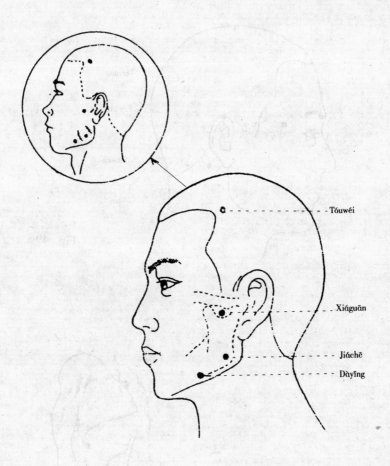

Fig. 51

198

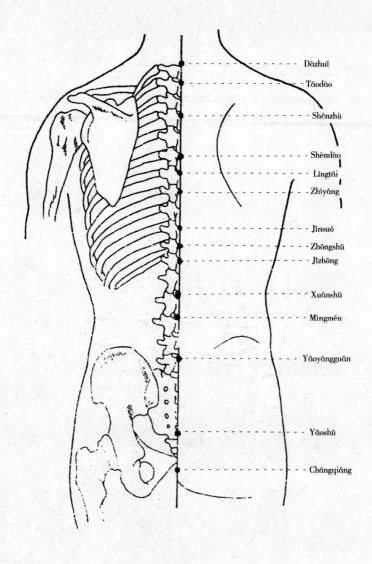

Dàzhuī
Táodào
Shēnzhù
Shèndào
Língtái
Zhìyáng
Jīnsuó
Zhōngshū
Jǐzhōng
Xuánshū
Mìngmén
Yāoyángguān
Yāoshū
Chángqiáng

Fig. 52

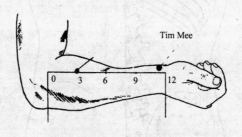

Fig. 53

图书在版编目(CIP)数据

100 种疾病的独穴疗法:英文/陈德成著.
—北京:外文出版社,2001
ISBN 7 - 119 - 02744 - 1

Ⅰ.1… Ⅱ.陈… Ⅲ.穴位疗法-英文 Ⅳ.R245.9

中国版本图书馆 CIP 数据核字 (2000) 第 72402 号

编　审　徐明强
责任编辑　余冰清
封面设计　王　志

外文出版社网址:

http://www.flp.com.cn

外文出版社电子信箱:

info@flp.com.cn

sales@flp.com.cn

100 种疾病的独穴疗法

陈德成　著

(美)Linda Gale　英文审阅

*

©外文出版社

外文出版社出版

(中国北京百万庄大街 24 号)

邮政编码 100037

通县大中印刷厂印刷

中国国际图书贸易总公司发行

(中国北京车公庄西路 35 号)

北京邮政信箱第 399 号　邮政编码 100044

2001 年(大 32 开)第 1 版

2001 年第 1 版第 1 次印刷

(英)

ISBN 7 - 119 - 02744 - 1/R·184(外)

05000

14 - E - 3421P